Praise for
Doctor Dealer

"An intensely absorbing look at the hubris of criminals."

—*San Francisco Book Review*

"An entertaining story with broad appeal."

—*Library Journal*

Greed.

Murder.

Drugs.

A deadly combination that led to murder and suicide.

Other books by George Anastasia

Blood and Honor: Inside the Scarfo Mob—the Mafia's Most Violent Family

Mobfather: The Story of a Wife and Son Caught in the Web of the Mafia

The Goodfella Tapes

The Summer Wind: Thomas Capano and the Murder of Anne Marie Fahey

The Last Gangster

Gotti's Rules: The Story of John Alite, Junior Gotti, and the Demise of the American Mafia

Other books by Ralph Cipriano

Target: The Senator: A Story about Power and Abuse of Power

The Hit Man: A True Story of Murder, Redemption and the Melrose Diner

Courtroom Cowboy: The Life of Legal Trailblazer Jim Beasley

DOCTOR DEALER

A doctor high on greed,
a biker gang high on opioids, and
the woman who paid the ultimate price

GEORGE ANASTASIA
AND
RALPH CIPRIANO

BERKLEY

New York

BERKLEY
An imprint of Penguin Random House LLC
penguinrandomhouse.com

ISBN: 9780593197622

The Library of Congress has catalogued the Berkley hardcover edition of this book as follows:

Names: Anastasia, George, author. | Cipriano, Ralph, author.
Title: Doctor dealer : a doctor high on greed, a biker gang high on opioids, and
the woman who paid the ultimate price / George Anastasia and Ralph Cipriano.
Description: First edition. | New York : Berkley, 2020. | Includes index.
Identifiers: LCCN 2019059055 (print) | LCCN 2019059056 (ebook) |
ISBN 9780593097762 (hardcover) | ISBN 9780593097779 (ebook)
Subjects: LCSH: Kauffman, James, -2018. | Kauffman, April, -2012. |
Murder for hire--New Jersey--Case studies. | Motorcycle gangs--New Jersey--Case
studies. | Medication abuse--New Jersey--Case studies.
Classification: LCC HV6533.N3 A53 2020 (print) | LCC HV6533.N3 (ebook) |
DDC 364.152/3092--dc23
LC record available at https://lccn.loc.gov/2019059055
LC ebook record available at https://lccn.loc.gov/2019059056

Berkley hardcover edition / September 2020
Berkley trade paperback edition / October 2021

Printed in the United States of America
1st Printing

DOCTOR DEALER

PROLOGUE

Journalism in its purest sense is the search for the truth. That search involves gathering as many facts as possible from as many different sources as can be found. But reporters who have been at the game for a while understand that knowing the facts doesn't necessarily mean you know the truth.

The murder of April Kauffman, which occurred on May 10, 2012, is a case in point.

Freddy Augello, a scruffy former boss of an outlaw biker gang known as the Pagans, was convicted in October 2018 of orchestrating the murder of the vivacious South Jersey radio host, who was found shot to death in the bedroom of the home she shared with her husband, Dr. James Kauffman, an endocrinologist.

The verdict was pretty much a slam dunk. The jury, which had heard testimony for about two weeks, took a little more than two hours to find Augello guilty of every charge he faced in the high-profile case.

A few months later, he was sentenced to life plus thirty years.

"I'm not John Gotti," the ponytailed sixty-two-year-old biker said in a lengthy and rambling statement in which he denied any involvement in the murder and in a drug ring he was convicted of heading.

Ordinarily a conviction and sentencing would signal the end of the story.

But there is nothing ordinary about the April Kauffman murder case.

April and James Kauffman had been married for a little more than ten years when she was killed. April, according to her adult daughter and many of her friends, was not happy in her marriage and wanted out. April also slept around. She had asked her husband several times for a divorce. He refused.

James Kauffman was a doctor with patients who loved and respected him. At the same time, he was a liar and a spendthrift who used his medical practice to generate tens of thousands of dollars in illegal income. He was running a pill mill with Augello and the Pagans, writing bogus prescriptions for the opioid oxycodone that the bikers sold on the streets. He was also a player in two lucrative insurance-fraud schemes, one of which generated tens of millions of dollars in illegal income for those involved.

But the good doctor never had to answer for any of that.

In January 2018, three weeks after being charged with paying Augello $50,000 to have April killed, James Kauffman committed suicide. He hanged himself in his jail cell.

The triggerman hired by Augello to carry out the murder also turned up dead. Originally it was thought he died of a drug overdose. Now authorities are trying to determine whether he was murdered.

For nearly five years, the investigation into April Kauffman's death went nowhere. The case was full of questions without answers. Facts without truth.

Journalists learn early in their careers that reporting is built around answers to the four Ws—"who," "what," "where" and "when." Those questions are answered with facts. But good stories are the ones that focus on the fifth W—"why." Sometimes facts are not enough to answer that question.

After two years of research that included sitting through the Augello trial, interviewing key players in the story, reviewing hundreds of pages of investigative documents and listening to hours of recorded conversations, we continue to wrestle with that fifth W.

This book is based on all the information available. The story is fortified by extensive interviews with two individuals whose lives were changed as a result of what happened to April Kauffman.

Andrew Glick, a member of the Pagans and onetime close friend of Freddy Augello, has spent hours sitting in a diner in South Jersey recounting his story. The six-foot, two-hundred-twenty-pound outlaw biker was a key government witness in the case, agreeing to secretly record conversations with Augello and others while working with authorities.

He stepped out of the biker underworld following his arrest in November 2017 on drug-dealing and weapons charges. Looking at forty years in prison, he said the choice to cooperate was easy. Glick, who had a Pagan's Motorcycle Club tattoo that stretched from his right shoulder to his elbow, was self-deprecating and matter-of-fact as he detailed his life as a biker and his lucrative career as a meth and cocaine distributor. Those were part-time jobs, he explained. He worked forty hours a week in a real job. He was a chef.

Not exactly the stereotypical motorcycle gangbanger, Glick owned rental properties and lived in a sprawling $300,000 house on seven partially wooded suburban acres with his wife and two dogs just outside of Atlantic City, New Jersey. There was a swimming pool in the backyard, along with several out-buildings, including a garage where he worked on motorcycles and a large shed that served as a biker clubhouse.

His marriage was breaking up at the time of his arrest, he said, in part because he had brought his girlfriend home to live in the house he shared with his wife.

"I think I crossed the line when I did that," he said with a shrug.

"You think?" he was asked. "You brought your girlfriend home to live in the same house as your wife?"

"It was a big house," he said.

Carole Weintraub moved in a world far removed from Andrew Glick's. She resides in a glass-walled condo worth more than one million dollars that overlooks a ritzy stretch of South Broad Street known as the "Avenue of the Arts" in Center City Philadelphia. Her social life included concerts at the nearby Academy of Music and dinners at the exclusive Union League. The American University– and Villanova-educated executive recruiter had been James Kauffman's girlfriend when they attended Atlantic City High School in the 1970s. They had grown up just a mile away from each other in identical one-story beach bungalows. Both were children of hardworking Jewish parents. Both of their fathers were in the bar business. They broke up during her second year in college.

Forty years later, after hearing about April Kauffman's murder from a friend who had read about it in a newspaper, Carole sent "Jimmy" a letter of condolence. A month later they were dating. A year later they were married.

Carole Weintraub offers a unique look at the murder case. She came into it after the fact, but with prior knowledge of who James Kauffman was. Or at least who she thought he was. She has spent the years since her late husband's arrest trying to find the truth. She has many facts, but just as many unanswered questions.

Sitting in her apartment, twenty stories above Center City, with Esther, her pet Brussels griffon, plopped on her lap, Carole Weintraub said she was on a mission.

"I want answers," she said. "I need answers. I want to know how he got involved with the people he got involved with. I want to know what happened in his life to make him do the things he did."

The thoughts, insights and speculation offered by Andrew Glick and Carole Weintraub help paint a picture that may come closer to the truth than the facts gathered by investigators, reporters and Internet conspiracy theorists who continue to write about the case.

James Kauffman was a master at compartmentalizing his

life. Carole Weintraub saw one part of him; Andrew Glick, another. Their views, their perspectives, their interactions with the doctor form the backdrop for this story. Today neither can say with certainty that they knew who Jim Kauffman was. They saw only what he wanted them to see. He spent his life creating personas. He was a gifted physician who cared deeply for his patients. He was an arrogant control freak who insisted on doing things his way. He was a charming socialite. He was a drug dealer. He was a loving husband. He was a power-hungry and violent narcissist who thought he could get away with murder.

And even in death, he continued to create his own narrative.

His suicide note, six pages handwritten on a yellow legal pad and left on his prison bed, provides a fitting ending to this story, but like so much else in this case, it raises more questions than it answers.

ONE

The murder was carried out with cold-blooded efficiency. April Kauffman was asleep in the bedroom she no longer shared with her husband in their stately two-story home on Woodstock Drive in Linwood, New Jersey, an upper-middle-class neighborhood just outside of Atlantic City. It was a little after five a.m. on May 10, 2012. Her husband, Dr. James Kauffman, was downstairs getting ready to leave for work. He was an endocrinologist with a lucrative practice in a busy office less than a fifteen-minute drive from their home.

The doctor, as he did almost every morning, would stop at a Wawa, a local convenience store, on his way to work. The store was a few blocks from their house. The security camera in place at the Wawa would capture him that morning entering and leaving the store.

This, investigators would later determine, was just a few

minutes after he had handed the hit man a gun and pointed to his wife's upstairs bedroom.

"She's up there," he said.

Several hours later a handyman who worked for the Kauffmans would discover April's body sprawled on the floor next to her bed. She had been shot twice. One bullet had shattered her elbow. The other had ripped through her side, slicing through a lung, her heart and her other lung. A medical examiner would speculate that she struggled out of bed after being shot, then collapsed on the floor. She had bled to death internally, he said, estimating that at least two liters of blood had poured from her wounds.

The hit man was later identified as Francis "Frank" Mulholland. He was a junkie and, it would turn out, he was ill suited for the job. But he had been offered $10,000 to commit the murder. That was enough to satisfy his habit for several months. He was driven to the home that morning by Joseph "Irish" Mulholland. They shared the same last name, but were not related. Joe Mulholland said he dropped Frank off near the house in the dark that morning and told him he would be waiting for him a few blocks away. He was driving a white Silverado pickup truck.

Joe Mulholland would later describe himself as a reluctant getaway driver.

Reluctant and also guilt ridden.

Although it would be nearly five years before law enforcement would put the case together, there were rumors, hints and whispers from day one. James Kauffman wanted his wife dead. He had talked to more than a few people about this. There was word in the Atlantic County underworld, particularly in the underworld populated by outlaw biker gangs, that there was a doctor willing to pay to have his wife killed.

Murder, the good doctor had decided, was cheaper than divorce.

At the time, the Kauffmans were a celebrity couple in Atlantic County. He was a dapper, wealthy physician who spoke at symposiums and who railed against the dietary habits and sedentary lifestyle of patients battling diabetes. This was the bulk of his practice. Described by some as charismatic and by others as arrogant, the doctor was hands-on both in practicing medicine and in a lifestyle that was luxurious and indulgent. He was an enthusiastic gun collector. He had an array of rifles and handguns that he kept under lock and key in his home. He spent time skeet shooting and on firing ranges. He was also a motorcycle enthusiast. In addition to his home in Linwood, he kept a vacation home in Arizona for getaways. April was his second wife. For those who liked to converse in stereotypes, she was the shiksa blond bombshell who had swept the much older doctor off his feet. She was forty-seven at the time she was killed. He was sixty-two.

They had been married for ten years. It was her third marriage. Her second husband had also been a doctor. Their divorce had been somewhat tumultuous. April had a grown daughter, Kim Pack, from her first marriage. Pack would later provide investigators with key pieces of information. From day one, she was suspicious if not convinced that James Kauffman had had something to do with her mother's death.

April Kauffman had created a life for herself that few would have expected given her background. She had had what a friend would later describe as a "somewhat unsettled childhood," raised by her grandmother and separated from four siblings that her mother had placed in foster care. She emerged as someone who was constantly looking for validation and, more important, for love. That search would continue as an adult. She owned and operated a beauty salon and had an interest in a restaurant-catering business. April was vivacious and outgoing, with flowing blond hair and a flirtatious manner; her upbeat personality was often a mask that hid insecurity and self-doubt.

At the time of her death, she had a weekly radio show in At-lantic County and had become a strong advocate for the rights of military veterans. "She was part princess, part bulldog," said an associate who worked with her on veterans' issues. That work brought her into contact with elected officials and government and military leaders in the area. Among other things, every Thanksgiving she would host a dinner at her home for recruits from the US Coast Guard station in nearby Cape May, young men and women who were unable to be with their families. She was offering a home away from home during the holiday.

Friends and neighbors would be invited as well. One local man who was a regular at the dinners had created something of a problem, according to an account provided by her daugh-ter. He was a cross-dresser who would show up in drag. April had no problem with his proclivities, but told him some of the recruits were uncomfortable. She said that while he was wel-come to come, she would prefer that he show up dressed as a man. It wasn't a question of her being intolerant, but rather a typical attempt on her part to ensure that her guests were at ease in her home.

In her last radio appearance, she described herself in terms that would prove to be a fitting epitaph. "I don't like training wheels," she said. "That's why . . . I drive a Corvette. I drive a motorcycle. I'm a full-throttle person."

On that same radio show, she also offered this eerie commentary: "I feel like I'm on borrowed time. And now if I was to be taken out, I'm telling you going up to see our Creator, I know I raised my daughter right with right American values. . . . She's moral. She's a good person, a hard worker, a patriotic person. . . ."

April Kauffman was well-liked and highly regarded in business, social and political circles around South Jersey, and her murder sent shock waves through those communities for various reasons, some of them unspoken.

"She was a do-gooder," said one person familiar with the events that unfolded. "But she had a voracious sexual appetite. The doctor thought he was a swinger, but his wife, she was major-league."

The sexual lifestyle of April and James Kauffman would hang over the murder investigation. In fact, there are those who believe one of the reasons the case went cold for so long was pressure from powerful individuals to keep details about April's sexual partners—some of whom moved in the upper circles of government, politics and business—from becoming public. April kept a diary. But after she was murdered, it disappeared.

Its content might have provided answers to what happened to her and why. Among other things, it might have shown how much she knew about her husband's involvement in a pill mill ring linked to an outlaw motorcycle gang. Medical records from

Dr. Kauffman's office would show that he was writing prescriptions for oxycodone for members and associates of the Pagans, a motorcycle gang that dominated the biker underworld in the Philadelphia–South Jersey region. In fact, there are those who would describe the Pagans as one of the toughest and most violent gangs on the East Coast. Several years earlier the Pagans had waged war against the Hells Angels, who attempted but failed to move into Pagan territory in Philadelphia and New Jersey.

Dr. Kauffman liked to identify with the bikers, although he had little in common with most of them. "People like us," he would say while discussing the biker world with a member of the club. The club member would nod, but would later shake his head.

"He didn't have a fuckin' clue what we were about," the biker said.

Jim Kauffman liked to portray himself as a tough guy. He would refer to his experience with an elite Green Beret Army unit and to his two tours of duty in Vietnam. He would sometimes show up in Army fatigues and a beret while supporting his wife's veterans' advocacy programs. He occasionally filled in on or cohosted her radio show. His military background, friends would say, was one of the things that drew April to the older man she would eventually marry. Part of his story was detailed in a paper written by April's daughter, Kim, when she was a college student. The assignment was to interview a military veteran. The interview took place shortly after April and Jim had married. He told a detailed story about how his unit had come under a vicious attack by the Vietcong and about how he had been one of the few to survive, licking water off leaves as he struggled to make his way out of the jungle.

None of it was true.

He had never been in the military.

About a year before she was killed, April discovered the lie. Those who knew her said it was one of the reasons she wanted a divorce. Authorities also would claim it was one of the reasons she was murdered. A law enforcement affidavit written five years after the homicide included the claim that about a year before she was killed "April became aware that Doctor Kauffman had never served in the Armed Forces and was not a veteran in any capacity. It is known that April was devastated by this revelation and it is believed that she threatened to use this info to produce a beneficial divorce from him."

Authorities would also claim that she was threatening to expose his involvement in the pill mill operation. But there is little to support that allegation or that she even knew about the oxycodone ring.

The pill mill, in fact, was only a small piece of the doctor's criminal activity.

Federal authorities had linked him and another local doctor, along with the representative of a pharmaceutical company, to a massive insurance-fraud scheme that involved prescribing compound-cream prescriptions for pain management. Compound cream, scams based on which have played out across the country, has been described as the "snake oil of the twenty-first century" by an insurance watchdog group. Like the pill mill operation and the opioid crisis it helped fuel, fraudulent scripts for unneeded creams to treat nonexistent pain was another example of Dr. James Kauffman trading his medical ethics—first do no harm—for dollars.

He also was targeted in a separate insurance-fraud scheme involving unnecessary blood tests. He would prescribe a test and, investigators later alleged, he would receive a kickback from the lab that conducted the procedure and billed the patient's insurance company. Both the compound-cream and blood-test scams generated tens of thousands of dollars in illegal income for the doctor, authorities now believe. This was in addition to his legitimate income from what has been described as a thriving and highly regarded medical practice, fees he was paid for speaking engagements at pharmaceutical conventions and, of course, the cash he made in the pill mill operation.

Money, it appears, was more important than the practice of medicine for Dr. James Kauffman. Or, perhaps, it was that he viewed the practice of medicine as a conduit for cash. So when he balked at granting April a divorce, telling friends and associates there was no way he was going to give her "half of his empire," she launched a counterattack.

She was burning up his credit cards, several of which were close to maxing out. Thousands had been spent on furnishing a home they shared in Tucson, Arizona, and now she was planning a $60,000 kitchen renovation for the home in Linwood. The credit card bills that arrived each month were her way of pressuring her husband into letting her go. She hoped he would come to the conclusion that it would be cheaper to divorce her.

He decided it would be even cheaper to have her killed.

Dr. Kauffman's net worth at the time was an estimated

$4.6 million, according to authorities. The doctor believed April would be in line for half of that in a divorce settlement. So he put out word in the biker underworld that he was willing to pay to have her killed. The price varied depending on whom he was talking with, but the range was between $10,000 and $50,000. Even at the high end, the doc considered it a bargain.

A security surveillance camera mounted on the wall of Mainland Regional High School about a block from the Kauffman home recorded traffic passing by in the early-morning hours of May 10, 2012. Shortly after five a.m. a Silverado pickup truck, like the one Irish Mulholland said he was driving that morning, passed by. A few minutes later an SUV like the Ford Explorer driven by Dr. Kauffman took the same route. That same SUV would be filmed in the parking lot of the Wawa convenience store a few minutes later.

Finally, several minutes after the SUV had been picked up by the high school surveillance camera, a man was spotted walking by. He was wearing white sneakers, dark sweatpants and a dark hoodie. Although there was no way to see it on camera, the man was also carrying a gun. Frank Mulholland, minutes after the death of April Kauffman, was recorded fleeing from the scene.

That was when the cold, efficient hit began to unravel.

The hit man got lost in suburbia. As dark turned to dawn and residents woke and began to emerge from their homes, Frank Mulholland wandered around the neighborhood, finally reconnecting with Joe "Irish" Mulholland, who had parked at a diner about a mile from the murder scene.

"He got disoriented, tried to cut through the high school

property and got lost," Irish would say later in explaining the reason it had been more than an hour before they reconnected. "He called me on his cell and said, 'Where are you?' I told him I was at the diner."

Irish Mulholland had originally parked in front of a paint store closer to the crime scene. He was a painter by trade. His business was Custom Design Painting. There was a bagel shop across the street, and while he waited, he walked over to the store and bought a bagel that he sat eating in the cab of his pickup truck as April Kauffman lay bleeding to death on the floor of her bedroom.

Irish said he decided it was not smart to park in front of a closed business at that time of the morning.

"I was sitting there, waiting and waiting," he said. "I didn't want the cops to get suspicious."

So he drove to the Point Diner and parked there instead. That was where he was when Frank Mulholland called and that was where they reconnected.

Once inside the cab of the pickup truck, Frank told Irish, "The job is done."

Irish fired up the engine of his truck and pulled out of the diner parking lot. He would take Route 9 toward the Villas, a community in lower Cape May County where Frank Mulholland lived.

In the cab of the pickup, Frank talked about the murder. He said that the woman had screamed when he walked into the bedroom and that he had put two bullets in her head, the first of many conflicting accounts of how the murder of April Kauffman had gone down. Irish Mulholland used his cell phone to make a call as he drove Frank home. The call was to Ferdinand "Freddy" Augello, a leader of the Pagans and the man Jim Kauffman had paid to have his wife killed. Irish Mulholland had Augello's number on speed dial. Their conversation that morning was brief and to the point.

"It's done," Mulholland said he told Augello.

"Okay," he said Augello replied.

Then Mulholland pushed the end-call button.

On the half-hour drive to the Villas, Frank showed Irish the gun and also pulled a wad of money from his pocket. It was $10,000 in cash, money he had been paid to kill April Kauffman. He peeled off a thousand and handed the money to Irish.

A few days later, Irish said he met Frank, and they talked about what had happened. The hit man junkie, he said, was angry at himself and "disgusted" by what he had done.

"I fucked up," Frank said.

Irish couldn't find the right words to reply.

"Well, you did it, man. I mean, it is what it is. You did it."

Frank Mulholland never recovered. He was "out on a bender for a year and a half after this," Irish Mulholland said.

Carole Weintraub heard about April Kauffman's death from a friend who had read about it in the newspaper the morning after it happened. A few days later, she sent a letter of condolence to Jim Kauffman, a man she had known years earlier. They had been high school sweethearts growing up in Atlantic City but had drifted apart after they both went off to college. Like Jim, she had married and divorced. Like Jim, she had had a successful career. She was a top-notch corporate recruiter, an executive headhunter. While she didn't realize it at the time, the condolence letter and her subsequent reconnection with Jim more than forty years after they had first dated would drag her into a world of drugs, sex, murder and betrayal that she still doesn't completely understand.

Andrew Glick heard about the murder when he returned home from work that afternoon. As he walked in the door of the home he shared with his wife, she said, "You won't believe it. I just saw on TV. Your doctor's wife was murdered." Glick, who worked as an executive chef at a senior citizen housing facility, was the president of the Cape May County chapter of the Pagan's Motorcycle Club at the time. He had succeeded Freddy Augello in that spot. Glick was also part of the pill mill operation and was aware of the doctor's desire to have his wife killed. In fact, Glick had turned down a murder-for-hire offer from Augello, and he knew several other members of the biker gang who also had rejected the proposal.

"It just wasn't something we would do," the barrel-chested and tattooed biker said later. "Killing a woman? For what? She wasn't part of our world. We don't do that." But Glick knew there would be consequences once authorities started to investigate the murder. "Oh, fuck," he said to himself as he watched the story on the television screen. "We're all going to jail."

TWO

Crime statistics in Linwood, New Jersey, are measured in single digits. Burglaries, robberies, rapes and assaults are rare in the upper-middle-class bedroom community located about nine miles west of Atlantic City. Murders are virtually unheard-of. April Kauffman's homicide was just the second to occur in the four-square-mile community in ten years.

The median family income in Linwood is about $103,000, according to 2010 census statistics. Most of the community's approximately seven thousand residents are white (about 93 percent) and many are professionals. A one-hundred-ten-acre private country club, which bills itself as one of South Jersey's "oldest and most respected private golf clubs" (individual membership fees range from $1,500 to $6,000), is located along Shore Road, one of the few major thoroughfares that crisscross the community. Mainland Regional High School, which receives students from Linwood and the nearby communities of Northfield and Somers Point, is the town's other major entity. A bedroom community in almost every sense of that term, Linwood avoided the tumult brought to the region when voters approved legalized casinos for Atlantic City back in 1976. Crime increased substantially in the boardwalk resort, but never filtered out to the suburbs. The burbs were the communities that reaped the benefits of the economic boom that the casino industry brought to the area. While high rollers and day-trippers poured into and out of Atlantic City on a regular basis and hookers turned parts of Pacific Avenue into an open-air brothel, suburban communities like Linwood managed to stay out of the fray. Its residents were the ones working the better jobs, receiving the higher pay and pursuing the professional careers that came with the blackjack tables, slot machines and roulette wheels.

In that sense, the April Kauffman murder was an aberration. This was not something that happened here, neighbors would tell one another. But it had. And the community was abuzz. The gossip, the rumors and the speculation that started that day out on the sidewalk would continue for the next six years. It would turn out that Andrew Glick's instincts were correct. In a matter of days, investigators were picking up information linking the Pagans to the murder of April Kauffman. They were also hearing stories about the rocky relationship between the doctor and his wife and reports that April Kauffman had told several people that her husband had threatened to kill her.

But it would be years before anyone was charged.

A series of reports filed by Detective Michael Mattioli paints a clear and intriguing picture of what authorities saw, heard and did in the early stages of the investigation. Mattioli, assigned to the Major Crimes Squad of the Atlantic County Prosecutor's Office, was one of the first on the scene and spent that day gathering evidence and taking statements.

He spoke on at least three occasions with Jim Kauffman, who told a story that would conflict in part with some things he would later claim. These discussions took place on the lawn outside the home as neighbors, curiosity seekers and the media gathered. Perhaps Jim Kauffman was too upset to get his story straight. Or perhaps what he said contained pieces of the truth. The sense from those who knew Jim Kauffman was that he always felt he was the smartest person in the room and was able to control or manipulate any situation to his advantage. With his wife dead on the floor of their bedroom, it was important for him to come across as the loving, grieving and shocked spouse.

Mattioli wrote that Kauffman described the last night he spent with his wife as a typical evening at home. He arrived first, around five thirty. April had done a radio show that afternoon, he told Mattioli, then stopped at Yesterday's, a local pub, with some friends from work. She got home around six. Jim Kauffman said he opened a bottle of wine and then cooked steaks on a grill. He and April spent some time in their hot tub, then went to bed, where they made love.

While he would later claim that he spent the night in bed with his wife, Mattioli said Kauffman told him that he moved to a separate bedroom because he snored and it would sometimes keep his wife awake. It was the first of several conflicting details as the doctor spun the story of his wife's last hours alive.

He said he watched part of a Phillies game on television before returning to the master bedroom to give his wife a kiss good night. April, he said, was sitting up in her bed, working on her laptop. He said he returned to the separate bedroom down the hall, where he watched some news on television before falling asleep. After waking in the morning, he showered and dressed. He left for work around five thirty a.m. His wife was sleeping soundly at that time, he said. He left by way of the garage. He said the front door was locked.

James Kauffman then recounted how he had stopped at the Wawa on his way to the hospital to pick up a newspaper. But the papers hadn't been delivered yet. At the hospital he checked to see if any of his patients had been admitted, then spent some time doing paperwork before heading to his office. He was at his office before seven a.m. Most of his office staff arrived around seven thirty.

After seeing several patients, Kauffman told Mattioli, he tried to contact April, calling home and calling her cell phone, but he got no answer. At nine thirty, he said, he put in a call to Billy Gonzalez, a handyman who did odd jobs around the house and was supposed to show up that morning to care for the parrots in the aviary that was located on the first floor of the house. Gonzalez would later tell authorities that he arrived a little before nine and entered through the front door, which was unlocked. In fact, it was later determined that April Kauffman frequently left the front door unlocked so that Gonzalez and others hired to do work around the house and grounds would have access.

Gonzalez confirmed that Dr. Kauffman called him twice

that morning. He said in the five years he had worked for the Kauffmans, he had never received a call from the doctor before. In fact, he said, the only times he had ever spoken to the doctor on the phone were when April would hand him the phone in the midst of a conversation she was having with her husband because the doctor wanted to tell Billy something about a job or chore that he wanted him to take care of.

The handyman described how he had approached April's bedroom after the doctor's second call and discovered her body sprawled on the floor. He called the doctor back and was told to call 911.

During the course of his interview, Gonzalez also told the detective about a bizarre message he had received early that morning. He said that when he awoke he had a text message from "Miss April."

The text had arrived at three twenty-seven a.m. and read simply, "See you in the AM."

Mattioli wrote that "Billy found the message strange for several reasons: First, he was just with April on the previous day, Wednesday May 9th, working at the house and going food shopping with her. That afternoon, April dropped him off at home @ 2:00pm on her way to her radio show in Ocean City. When she dropped him off, she told him that she would see him in the morning. Furthermore, every Thursday he worked for the Kauffmans at their house and if they wanted him to work other days, April would call him to see if he was available. Finally, Billy stated it was not normal for April to text him at night, stating she never texted him past 10 pm (never in the middle of the night) and it was always about what she needed him to do."

That text message would add fuel to what would later become one of the many conflicting murder theories in the case. Was April Kauffman already dead when the alleged hit man, Frank Mulholland, entered the house? Had her husband shot her earlier that morning and then sent the text on her laptop to cover his tracks and support his own alibi? That theory would surface later, but on day one of the investigation, the early-morning text message was just a strange and quirky piece of information that didn't appear to have any relevance. For the most part, Gonzalez's account conformed to the story James Kauffman told authorities that day.

Dr. Kauffman said he rushed home from the office after telling Gonzalez to call for help. He said when he entered the home and rushed up the stairs, he stopped short. His wife, he said, was lying on the floor of the bedroom. He knew she was dead.

"I asked him if she felt cold when he touched her," Mattioli wrote in his report of his first interview with Kauffman. "Kauffman said he never entered the bedroom or touched his wife, adding, 'Detective, I am a doctor and have seen enough dead bodies to know when someone is dead.'" Kauffman would later change this story, claiming he had felt for his wife's pulse. That, he said, was how he had known she was dead.

Mattioli said after the medical examiner arrived at the scene and determined that April had died of gunshot wounds, he went outside and spoke to the doctor again, telling him his wife had been shot. Kauffman would claim that he only heard rumors that his wife had been shot and that it would be weeks before he knew for certain that was the cause of death. Mattioli also said he was waiting for a search warrant and asked what of value was in the house. Kauffman told him his wife had jewelry valued at about a half-million dollars and that he had "an extensive gun collection."

The detective said Kauffman was going to a neighbor's house and left a cell phone number at which he could be reached. Kauffman was told he would not be able to enter his residence until a search had been completed and the crime scene fully examined.

Several hours later, Mattioli said, he was informed that the doctor was back outside and wanted to speak with him. Mattioli said that he went outside and that the doctor asked if the detective could get him something from inside the house. Mattioli said that would depend on what it was.

"He asked me if I could get him a bottle of Canadian Club whiskey and a bottle of sweet vermouth located in the first-floor bar area," Mattioli wrote in his report. The detective said he turned down the request.

Later, Mattioli said the doctor asked for and was given his wallet and heart-medication tablets, which were in the cabin of his Ford Explorer. The detective also noted some final comments Jim Kauffman made to him that night after learning that he would not be able to get back into his home and would probably have to spend the night in a hotel or with friends.

"I called . . . to tell him we were still processing the scene and we would be holding it overnight to continue in the morning," Mattioli wrote. "Kauffman jokingly asked what time I would be picking him up to take him to a hotel. I apologized for the inconvenience. He said he hoped all his requests hadn't been a problem. I told him he had not been a problem, [to] which he responded, 'If I had been, I'd be in handcuffs already. . . . By the way, detective, if you ever have to put handcuffs on me, be careful. I have a very bad shoulder.'"

Less than twelve hours after finding his wife dead on the floor of their bedroom, James Kauffman was joking with the lead detective charged with finding out who had killed her. The doctor would eventually be put in handcuffs, but Mattioli would no longer be involved in the investigation by the time that happened.

The detective, however, did gather crucial pieces of evidence in the early stages of the probe—evidence that wasn't acted on until later, but that nevertheless helped build the case against Jim Kauffman and Freddy Augello.

One tantalizing piece of information came after Mattioli astutely checked phone records to determine the origins of the phone calls from Kauffman to the handyman Billy Gonzalez that morning. Dr. Kauffman claimed he was calling from his office at eleven twenty-five when he asked Gonzalez to check on his wife. Gonzalez called back at eleven twenty-six and told Dr. Kauffman that his wife was on the floor, unconscious. That was when Kauffman told the handyman to call 911. But by checking cell tower location pinpoints, the detective was able to determine that the doctor was within a block or two of his home when those two calls were made. In effect, the detective wrote, Kauffman was around the corner from his home when the 911 call went out. "At the time of these two calls," Mattioli wrote, "Kauffman was geographically within blocks of his home as he directed Billy Gonzalez to locate April."

Jim Kauffman was already on his way to, in fact had practically arrived at, what he knew was a murder scene when he told

Gonzalez to check on his wife and when he told him to call for help.

This would also be consistent with the report of a neighbor, Millie Tate, who was interviewed by Mattioli on July 2, seven weeks after the murder.

Millie Tate said she was pulling out of her driveway on her way to work that morning when Jim Kauffman drove by at a high speed. She said the doctor never drove like that. She said she had pulled out of her driveway and was headed up the street when she saw the flashing lights and heard the sirens of a police car and an ambulance in the distance heading her way. She told Mattioli that she decided to turn around and head back toward home, concerned that something had happened at the Kauffmans'. There she saw Jim Kauffman, who had pulled into the driveway of the home, sitting in the cab of his Ford Explorer. At first, she said, he appeared to be talking on the phone. Then he got out and stood behind the vehicle, looking down the street. As the police car and ambulance approached, she said, he sprinted into the house. She said he slammed the door of the Explorer closed as he ran by and rushed through the front door of his house.

A few minutes later, she said, she saw the doctor come out of the house and collapse on the lawn. She went over to him and asked what was wrong.

Without looking at her, he said, "April's dead."

Tate told Mattioli that she and April had grown close over the years that they were neighbors and that April had often discussed her marital woes with her. She said April told her she wanted to leave her husband and had asked many times for a divorce. Once, about five years earlier, she said April showed her what she said were bullet holes in the dining room floor, claiming Jim had shot up the floor during a heated argument. Millie Tate told Mattioli that April was afraid of her husband and had told her, "If I get killed . . . he did it."

Given what Mattioli was learning about the Kauffman marriage, the incident described by Tate could have been related to any one of dozens of domestic altercations that marked what Kim Pack described as the "tumultuous" relationship between her mother and stepfather. Millie Tate said April believed her husband was having an affair. Jim Kauffman repeatedly denied this in the aftermath of his wife's death.

April, on the other hand, was less than faithful on several occasions. Her daughter, Kim Pack, frankly admitted that her mother had had at least four affairs during her ten-year marriage to Jim Kauffman. Her paramours included a contractor working on their home in Arizona, a gardener who did work on the home in Linwood, an Atlantic County hospital executive and the twenty-two-year-old son of a doctor who was a close friend of Jim Kauffman's.

The incident with the twenty-two-year-old led to threats, a confrontation and a detailed report filed on June 4, 2006, by officers with the Egg Harbor Township police department. At the time, Jim Kauffman was in Cincinnati on a business trip/speaking engagement. The twenty-two-year-old had been hired by April to do work around the house and yard in Linwood. That Sunday afternoon, according to the police report, Kim Pack stopped by the house and walked in on her mother and the young man locked in an embrace on the couch.

"It's not what it seems!" the young man shouted as he bolted out of the room. Kim Pack left the house and later began to receive calls from her mother's young lover, who said he wanted to come over to her house to explain and apologize.

Kim Pack was nine months pregnant at the time. Her husband answered the door at their home and got into a confrontation with the young man. The Packs called the police. They also put in a call to Jim Kauffman, who later said he learned about the "situation" from his son-in-law.

Threats were made. Charges and countercharges were filed, including a report from the young man's father, the longtime friend of Jim Kauffman's. He said he had received a call from Kauffman, who was in Cincinnati but was returning home in two days.

The police officer who filed the report noted that the father of the young lover "explained to me that he and James Kauffman are best friends. He stated that he received a phone call from Kauffman at approximately 2205 hours. He stated that Kauffman, who is due home on Tuesday morning, stated that when he arrived home he was going to put a bullet in his wife [April Kauffman], he was then going to put a bullet in [his friend's] son . . . and that if he [the friend] stood in his way he would put a bullet in him also."

The police officer filing the report said he was also told that "Kauffman has a large gun collection and sometimes displays a temper."

That was part of the backstory floating around in social circles as the investigation into the murder of April Kauffman continued. By July of 2012 when Millie Tate told Mattioli of April's fears and concerns, the Major Crimes Squad detective and others working the case already had heard about a murder contract that had been put out on April's life by her husband.

In a report filed on June 2, Mattioli described an interview with a confidential informant who told him of a conversation he had had a few weeks before the homicide with a Pagan's Motorcycle Club member known as "Slasher." The informant said that Slasher told him about a doctor from Linwood who was writing "dirty scripts" for him. He said the doctor was "willing to pay a lot of money" to have his wife killed. The informant said he was told "it would be easy because the front door would be open and the victim would be asleep." The informant said Slasher asked him if he would be willing to commit the murder or if he knew anyone who would do it. The informant said he wasn't interested.

Based on that tip, Mattioli contacted gang unit investigators, who linked the nickname Slasher to Glenn Seeler. Authorities determined that Seeler lived with a woman named Cheryl Pizza. Using the Pagans connection as the jumping-off point, Mattioli checked the medical records in Jim Kauffman's practice and determined that Seeler, Andrew Glick and Paul Pagano, three members of the outlaw motorcycle club, were regularly receiving scripts for oxycodone. Seeler was also receiving prescriptions for Percocet. And three women, including Pizza, who were described to have "known Pagan associations" were also receiving scripts on a regular basis.

Less than two months after the murder of April Kauffman, investigators were connecting the dots that Andrew Glick had warned would lead authorities to his door and the doors of other members of the pill mill. Through the rest of the year and into 2013, authorities would continue to track those leads.

A key source of information was Kim Pack, who met repeatedly with Mattioli. Pack had told the detective on the day of the murder that she suspected her stepfather.

"I really need to talk to you," she said after approaching Mattioli at the crime scene, still uncertain what had happened to her mother, but convinced that James Kauffman was responsible. That day and in the days that followed she would lay out the case against her stepfather, telling Mattioli that her mother wanted to end the marriage, but that Kauffman had "threatened to go nuclear on our family" if she divorced him. She said her mother told her that Kauffman said, "If she left him, he would kill her."

In an hour-long statement recorded on May 30, 2012, Kim Pack restated all the things she had been telling investigators over the previous three weeks. Her information would serve as the framework for the case. Some of the events she had witnessed herself. Others she had heard about from her mother, who, she said, talked to her several times a day. Among other things, she said her mother had misread her husband's intent and told her not to worry about his threats.

"I'm fine," she said her mother told her at one point. "He doesn't have the balls to do that."

The marriage, she said, had been coming apart for years. The couple slept in separate beds. The fights and bickering were constant. In February, she said, her mother was livid when James Kauffman failed to buy her an anniversary gift—they had been married on February 14, 2002—but instead had spent $2,000 on a new gun.

She said her mother was beside herself with anger after learning that her doctor husband had used her name to write scripts for a ninety-day supply of "antipsychotic medication" that he was taking. Kim Pack said her mother thought her husband was going to a psychiatrist, but learned that he had stopped the sessions. Instead, it appeared, he had decided to self-medicate, using her name on the scripts.

"I gotta leave him," April Kauffman told her daughter. "I can't stand this anymore."

A friend, she said, had told her mother she had two options: stay and bleed him dry of his money or divorce him and get half of all he owned.

"She told me she would take half of his empire," Kim Pack told the detectives interviewing her, and she said her mother had asked for a divorce "multiple times." Each time, she said, Dr. Kauffman would threaten her.

On the morning when Pack learned her mother was dead, she said her first thought was that those threats had "come to fruition." And when Kauffman called her in a panic and told her, "Mom's dead, Mom's dead," her only reply to him was, "What have you done?"

Pack also detailed some of the things she heard and saw as funeral arrangements were being made, including Kauffman telling her on the Saturday morning after the murder, when she stopped by the house to pick up some of her mother's belongings, "I can't be arrested. If they arrest me I'm gonna kill myself."

But the most disconcerting comments were those she heard

as family members and friends were sitting shiva, the Jewish custom of mourning after a death. She said she never heard Kauffman speak of his wife or of who might have killed her. Instead, she remembered walking in on the middle of a conversation in which Jim Kauffman told some friends, "They don't have anything on me."

THREE

Andrew Glick's mind was racing as he processed what his wife had told him and what he had seen in the television news report. April Kauffman was dead. She had been murdered. Freddy had finally found someone to do it, he said to himself. But who? And how? More important, he thought it would only be a matter of time before the law was kicking in his door and the doors of a half dozen other members of the club.

"It never should have happened," he said. "I told Freddy it was stupid. But Freddy didn't listen. He wanted the money. He was always broke. This was a big score for him. He took fifty grand from the doc and paid that junkie ten grand. Probably promised him more, but he was never gonna pay it. That's how Freddy was."

Glick knew that was the way Freddy Augello operated.

Augello had taken the contract to have April Kauffman killed but Glick and anyone else who knew him knew that Freddy wasn't going to do the job himself. He was too smart for that. He would find somebody to do it. That's what he had promised the doc. He had boasted about his underworld connections with both outlaw bikers and the mob. He could get it done. In exchange, the doc had promised Freddy $50,000 and had agreed to write scripts for oxycodone that Freddy and those he brought into the pill mill operation were turning into cash.

Glick had gotten involved in the pill mill in December of 2011. He had heard about it from Glenn Seeler and said he wanted in. Seeler, the biker whose name had been mentioned in the informant report about the murder contract, contacted Augello and then got back to Glick. He told him his first "appointment" with Dr. James Kauffman was on the morning of December 31, a Saturday.

"He said he had spoken to Freddy, who had set up the appointment," Glick recalled. "He told me to bring my insurance information, and he also gave me one of Freddy's business cards. He said to show that to the doc as kind of an introduction. The appointment was at eight in the morning. I was there at seven fifty-nine."

No one else was in the office. Kauffman opened the door and let him in. Glick filled out some papers, and after a brief examination, Kauffman wrote out the scripts. Glick said Kauffman asked him how long he had been in the club and whether he had any rank. He also admired the Pagan's Motorcycle Club tattoo that stretched from Glick's right shoulder to his elbow.

Glick had a history of diabetes, which legitimized his visit.

He got a prescription for medication to treat that problem and also got a script for one hundred twenty 30 mg oxycodone tablets. He would continue to receive scripts and sell the pills for the next five years.

Three days later, Glick said, Augello stopped by his house and during a meeting in the basement explained the pill mill operation. Freddy told him, "The sky's the limit." At the time, Glick said he assumed this was a drug deal. But he quickly learned that Jim Kauffman wanted much more out of his relationship with the bikers.

As they sat in the basement of his home, Glick was told that the doctor was looking for somebody to kill his wife. He said Augello told him, "She's treating him like a piece of shit. . . . She's fucking every dude in the county. She's gonna take him for everything. She's divorcing his ass."

Augello asked Glick if he knew anybody who was "capable."

"Bring them to me, and I'll take care of you," Glick said Augello told him, adding that "we gotta get this done soon" because the doctor "is not going to, you know, just sit here and keep doing this forever and us not doing anything."

"The sooner, the better," Glick said he was told.

Glick told Augello he would see if he could come up with anyone, but later told authorities he never had any intention of getting involved in the murder of April Kauffman.

One of the misconceptions early in the investigation was that the Pagans had somehow forced the doc to take part in the pill mill and then had killed his wife because he was balking at writing any more scripts. That, in fact, would be one of the scenarios Jim Kauffman would lay out to his own lawyers.

But Glick and other members of the Pagans knew the murder of April Kauffman was the doctor's idea and the offer to write scripts, to set up the pill mill, was his way to lure Augello into the plot. Oxycodone and fifty grand were what Jim Kauffman was offering the biker in exchange for the murder of his wife. There was also a promise to set Augello up in business out in Arizona.

Augello, looking for a better life out West, agreed to the deal. But Glick never thought the murder would happen. In several conversations after that first meeting in his basement, Glick told Augello it was a crazy idea. And when the doc started complaining about how long it was taking to set up the hit, Glick told Augello not to worry about it.

"What can he do?" Glick said. "Just keep stringing him along. We'll blackmail the shit out of him."

At that point, Glick figured the Pagans had Dr. Jim Kauffman in their pocket. What was he going to do, run to the cops? What would he tell them? These guys promised to kill my wife, and now they're reneging on the deal? Jim Kauffman had nowhere to go.

That, at least, was the way Glick saw it.

In 2012, Fred Augello was making five or six grand a month in the pill mill scam. Glick was bringing in about two grand. Not great money, but he had other sources of income, a legitimate job and serious cash from meth and cocaine sales. Augello, even with the pill mill money, was struggling financially. He had a half-assed sign-painting and graphic-artist business that he ran out of a garage, he repaired and built guitars and he played in a rock-and-roll and blues band called Who Dat. None of those ventures generated much cash. The murder contract was a serious payday for Augello. He also saw the offer to relocate to Arizona as a chance to turn his life around. All he had to do was arrange the murder of April Kauffman.

So while it is accurate to say that April was a victim of the opioid crisis that was tearing America apart, the actual cause of her death was greed. Both Kauffman and Augello were trying to protect "their empires," a county prosecutor would later tell a jury. Freddy Augello wanted her dead so he could collect the fifty grand and start a new life in Arizona. And Jim Kauffman wanted her dead so that he could keep all of his $4.6 million estate.

"Fifty thousand to kill a woman?" Glick asked. "That's not a lot of money. I wouldn't do it. But Freddy . . . he never had any money. So . . ."

Andrew Glick knew how Freddy's mind worked.

Augello was his onetime mentor and the guy most responsible for bringing him into the Pagans. Freddy's nickname in the club was "Miserable," which said all you needed to know about the guy. Augello was in his fifties when Glick met him. And it was clear his life had not turned out the way he had hoped. Whenever he could, he took it out on those around him. He made a living out of his sign-painting business but his passion was music. A wannabe rock star, he played in a band that his cousin had formed and he sat in on gigs whenever and wherever he could. The band would hustle for spots at local bars and restaurants, sometimes playing in the smaller rooms at some of Atlantic City's casinos. Freddy, with a graying ponytail that stretched to his waist and a scraggly goatee, was a poor man's

Keith Richards. He played guitar and sang. Loved performing and by his own account was more than just a "garage musician."

"I am not a third-rate guitar player," he said in response to a magazine article that, in passing, raised questions about his musicianship.

Whatever his ability, a friend said, "He didn't like to practice."

Augello had attended Holy Spirit High School, the regional parochial secondary school for Atlantic County. In the notes under his 1975 graduation picture in the school yearbook, Augello had indicated that he wanted to "become an artist or professional racer." Those notes also showed he had participated in crew and was president of his class during his freshman year. But he had drifted from job to job after high school and eventually settled into a less-than-lucrative lifestyle, hustling for a buck while becoming more and more involved in the biker underworld. It gave him a sense of belonging and also access to women. Freddy Augello always had a way with the ladies. He played off the bad-boy image that grew out of his biker and rock-and-roll personas. He looked and acted like a 1960s hippie but with a tough-guy attitude. There were chicks who loved it.

When they first met around 2001, Glick said that Augello was a bulky biker boss with a reputation. Glick had moved to Atlantic County from Wilmington, Delaware, where he had been born and raised. He rode a Harley and knew some Pagans from the Wilmington area. One was a friend from childhood.

"We played in the sandbox together," Glick said.

The Pagans had been a part of his life from the time he was

a teenager. He was the youngest of five children and grew up in the Richardson Park section of Wilmington, Delaware. His father and mother, he says, "were functioning alcoholics." His mother had been married four times, twice to the man he thought was his father. On her deathbed, he said, his mother told him who his real father was. He was a local fireman. Glick has vague memories of being brought as a small child to a firehouse where he was treated like a special guest. But that was when he was just two or three years old. He has no memories of connecting with the man as he grew older.

When he was eighteen Glick bought his first Harley with money he had earned working as a kitchen worker and short-order cook in burger joints. The jobs provided cash for the bike and also led to his career as a chef. Although he had scored over 1200 on his SAT, he wasn't interested in going to college. A high school counselor suggested cooking school and put him on to Johnson & Wales, a prestigious culinary institute in New England. The man he thought was his father was dead by then, but his mother helped pay the tuition. She died during his first year in school, he said, and he had to drop out. He found work in restaurants and continued to ride his bike. He wasn't interested in joining a biker club even though he had the opportunity and the connections. Two of his elder sisters dated members of the Delaware branch of the Pagans. Guys on motorcycles were always around the house, guys named Gypsy and Terrible Tony and Tiny.

Tiny was Antonio Martines, a fearless, drug-dealing leader of the Delaware chapter. One of Glick's sisters married the brother of Tiny's wife, so there was a familial connection. Glick

remembers the funeral for Martines, the biker pomp and ceremony, the display of colors as Martines was laid to rest. This
was in 1984. Glick was nineteen years old.

"He got shot," Glick said of Martines.

Shot several times, in fact.

In February 1984, Martines was on the run, ducking a federal indictment for drug dealing—meth and heroin. The car he
was riding in was stopped by federal agents on a highway near
the Ohio–Pennsylvania border. Glick was working as a cook at
the time. He still remembers reading the newspaper stories and
hearing about it from friends of the family.

A UPI news account tells it best. Datelined Hubbard, Ohio,
the report opened with these lines: "A member of the Pagans
motorcycle gang being sought on drug charges was shot to
death . . . after he fired a machine gun at federal agents who
had stopped him on Interstate 80."

Martines opened fire on the agents through the rear window
of the car he was riding in. He blasted away with an Israeli-
made Uzi, according to the UPI account. The feds had apparently been tracking him from Ohio after a drug deal had gone
down. The account mentioned that a briefcase "'full of money'
was found in Martines' bullet-riddled automobile." Martines's
wife and another woman were in the vehicle but were not injured.

Martines, thirty-nine at the time of his death, was one of the
larger-than-life bikers around whom outlaw legend is built.

"He was about five foot five and probably weighed close to
five hundred pounds," Glick said. "That's why they called him
Tiny. I remember one time he ordered a pizza with everything

on it. And I mean everything: pepperoni, sausage, mushrooms, extra cheese, peppers. It was gigantic. And he ate the whole thing."

Some people grow up idolizing baseball or football players. For others it's movie stars and other celebrities. Andrew Glick looked up to bikers. But it wasn't until he moved to New Jersey that he became interested in joining a biker gang.

His first marriage ended in divorce after less than three years. Remarried a short time later, he and his second wife, Vicki, moved to Atlantic County in 1998. One of his older sisters, married to an Atlantic City police officer, was living in the area. Glick found work as a cook at the Sands and then at Caesars, two Atlantic City casino-hotels, and earned enough money to buy a small house. Over the years, his salary would increase. He left the casino industry in 2001 to work for an agency that provided food services for senior citizen living facilities. This was even better pay, but more important, it provided regular hours, which led to more time on his bike. He also was developing a "part-time job" as a drug dealer, moving small and later moderate quantities of cocaine and meth. Originally, he said, he sold small quantities of cocaine—known as eight balls—to cover the cost of his own cocaine habit.

Life was good.

And then he met Freddy Augello.

He had started hanging out at bars where bikers congregated. Soon he attracted the attention of local club members who were always looking for recruits and always leery of possible undercover police informants. Glick, who was slightly over six feet tall and at that time weighed a solid two hundred twenty pounds, looked like a biker, or like the kind of guy the feds or state police would use to infiltrate a club.

He first bumped into Augello in a bar outside of Ocean City called Uncle Mike's.

"He asked me who I was and where I was from," Glick recalled. "Didn't seem to like me very much. I mentioned the names of a couple of Pagans I knew from Delaware. The next time we were in a bar together, his attitude had changed. He said he had checked on me. Those guys in Delaware had vouched for me. I was okay."

Glick would see Freddy from time to time as he drifted deeper and deeper into the biker underworld. He joined the Long Riders, a local club, and then moved to the Tribe, which was a "support club" for the Pagans. Support club members pay fees in exchange for an affiliation with a major club. Glick said he paid $250 for a "patch" that showed he was part of a club that supported the Pagans. He said members of the Tribe also paid a $50 annual fee to the bigger outlaw club. In exchange for the affiliation, members of the Tribe would make themselves available to go on runs and provide bodies when a show of force was needed. Glick was with the Tribe for about three years.

Sex and drugs were part of the lifestyle. Pagans and their support club members would get together to party on a regular basis. Strippers, go-go dancers and straight-up hookers were often part of the entourage at biker rallies. The club would usually take over a local bar and motel for a weekend. The girls received an "appearance fee" from the club and would be required to kick back part of their earnings. During a good weekend, Glick said, a dancer might earn $500 or $600. If she turned tricks, she could come away with $3,000 or $4,000.

One of the best biker rallies in New Jersey was the annual Roar to the Shore, a biker extravaganza each September in Wildwood, New Jersey, a "family" resort town that tried to extend the season beyond Labor Day by becoming a venue for conventions and conclaves. The volunteer firemen of New Jersey descend on the town for one weekend in September, taking up rooms in the hotels and motels and filling the bars and restaurants that would otherwise be ready to shut down for the season. The Roar to the Shore took up another weekend with the same financial benefits for local businesses.

That was the life Glick was entering as he joined the biker clubs and worked his way up the ladder to membership with the Pagans. Along the way he got to know—and sometimes genuinely respect and admire—some of the members. They rode together, partied together and busted some heads together. All of that was part of the outlaw biker underworld. They were "one percenters" and proud of it.

The designation "one percenter" grew out of an infamous biker brawl back in 1947 in Hollister, California. This was around the time a group of military veterans, feeling like outcasts after returning home from World War II, began riding together. Initially they called themselves the Pissed Off Bastards of Bloomington, a small town in San Bernardino County where several of them lived. The arrest of a biker and the subsequent riot in Hollister led leaders of many motorcycle clubs at the time to decry the violence and to proclaim that those who took part in the melee were not part of the legitimate motorcycle-club world, but rather represented one percent of those who rode.

Biker gangs later seized on that comment, happily describing themselves as "one percenters." A year after the incident in Hollister, the Pissed Off Bastards changed their name, adopting one that had been popular with fighter pilots and bomber crews during the war. They called themselves Hells Angels.

The Pagans were founded twelve years later. The group traces its origins to Prince George's County in Maryland, where in 1959 a biker named Lou Dobkin organized the club. Members originally rode Triumphs, but soon switched to Harley-Davidsons, the bikes preferred by most outlaw gangs. It would be another decade before the Pagans began to make a name for themselves in underworld and law enforcement circles. By that time their leader was Joe "Satan" Marron and the club's base of operation was in Delaware County, Pennsylvania, just outside of Philadelphia. Club members wore their "colors"—denim jackets festooned with patches and insignias proclaiming their affiliation. The symbols included the head of the mythological Norse god Surtr, the fire giant warrior. Drugs, primarily meth, were a major source of income for the club. Southern New Jersey and rural Pennsylvania provided plenty of wooded hideaways where meth labs could be set up. Being a "cooker"—someone who knew how to manufacture meth in those makeshift labs—was one of the highest callings in the organization. Drug dealing, extortion, sex and violence were what being a Pagan was all about.

Andrew Glick shook his head as he talked about those days, which he had heard about as a kid. Times had changed, he said, even in the biker underworld.

"It used to be being a Pagan was your job," he said ruefully. "Today you have to have a job to be a Pagan."

Still, he wanted in. His chance came on New Year's Day in 2005. Glick, a member of the Tribe with aspirations to join the Pagans, solidified his standing with the bigger club by taking part in a brawl at the Woodshed Tavern in Burlington County, New Jersey, an hour's ride from Atlantic City. This was at a time when the Pagans were fighting off an attempt by the Hells Angels to move into the Philadelphia–South Jersey area, which had always been Pagans territory.

The Hells Angels were the oldest and, by reputation at least, the toughest outlaw motorcycle gang in the country. The Pagans were a smaller club concentrated primarily along the Interstate 95 corridor that ran through Maryland, Delaware, Pennsylvania and New Jersey. There were some Pagan clubs farther south and one or two in the Pittsburgh area, but the Mid-Atlantic region had always been the club's primary stomping ground. The Angels had opened a clubhouse in Philadelphia and were out recruiting new members, even trying to get some members of the Pagans to "patch over"—to switch allegiance.

On that New Year's Day, Glick was out riding with other members of the Tribe. It was an exceptionally warm day for January, a perfect day to be out on a bike. But their ride was interrupted when a club member got a call from a leader of the Pagans. They met in the parking lot of a local bar. Leaving their bikes and their colors behind, they piled into an SUV and a pickup truck and headed for the Woodshed. There were seven of them, two Pagans and five members of the Tribe. No guns. But one of the Pagans had a hickory stick, a thick wooden ax handle. Glick and the others were told three members of the Hells Angels were trying to recruit some new members in the bar, which was located on Route 72 near Pemberton, New Jersey. What followed would be known in the biker underworld as the day of "Bloodshed at the Woodshed."

Glick and his six associates walked into the bar. While none of them were wearing their biker colors—the jackets that would designate them as members of the Pagans or the Tribe—there was no mistaking why they were there. The three Hells Angels looked up and knew immediately what was about to go down.

"Everyone just started swinging," Glick said. "It started inside the bar, but we all ended up in the parking lot. That's when one of our guys grabbed the hickory stick and began swinging.

"He bashed one guy's head in," Glick said. "I heard the thump."

The fight ended as quickly as it started. Glick and his associates piled back into the SUV and pickup truck and drove away, leaving three Hells Angels and a few of their would-be recruits dazed and bleeding. One member of the Angels had to be emergency airlifted to a hospital in nearby Camden. He recovered in a few days, but not before he got a "get well" phone call at his hospital bed from a Pagan leader.

"How'd you like that hickory shampoo?" said the voice on the phone.

No one was arrested, but police linked the confrontation to the simmering battle between the Angels and the Pagans. Three weeks later at one thirty in the morning, a Hells Angel was shot and killed as he was driving away from a go-go bar in South Philadelphia. The ambush occurred near the Schuylkill Expressway. The Angel was driving in a pickup truck. Another member, a newly inducted recruit, was riding alongside the truck on his Harley. As they headed west, a white Chevy Suburban pulled up alongside them, and two shooters opened fire. The target was the biker, the new recruit. The Hells Angel in the pickup truck swerved to provide a shield for the biker. He was hit in the head as a barrage of bullets ripped through the cab of his truck, which crashed into a fence. The Chevy Suburban sped off.

The murder remains an open case for Philadelphia Police homicide detectives, who quickly linked the shooting to the ongoing battle between the two biker gangs. No one has been charged.

Glick said the shooting was a matter of one-upmanship.

"The leader of the Pagans in Philly heard about the Bloodshed at the Woodshed," Glick recalled. "He decided the guys in Philly had to do something to top that. He liked to say, 'We're Philamaniacs.' They ambushed those guys because they wanted to top what we had done."

Soon after the incident at the Woodshed, Glick was invited to prospect with the Pagans, the first step to becoming a full-fledged member. It was like being a pledge in a college fraternity. He jumped at the chance, even though it meant he'd do a lot of grunt work like polishing members' bikes and running errands. Most important, he always had to be available.

Every prospect had to carry a "bag" in which he stored the necessities of club members, he said. If a member asked for something and you didn't have it in your bag, you had a half hour to come up with the item. If you didn't produce, you might get "lumped up." More important, your chances of getting a full membership were diminished.

Glick kept a set of small hand tools in his bag along with condoms, Kotex tampons, chewing gum, cigarettes (assorted brands, menthol and regular), Tylenol, Advil and, because he knew the quirks of one arrogant member of the club, a small bag of vanilla wafer cookies.

"This guy could be a real pain in the ass," Glick recalled. "I found out he loved these vanilla wafers, and I put some in my bag. When he asked for them, I was ready."

In 2007, less than a year after he began prospecting, Glick was formally initiated into the club. He had hoped to join the Atlantic County chapter, but because of some internal bickering (one of the club's members blackballed his membership), Glick was invited by Augello to join the Cape May chapter, where Augello was president.

Glick had gotten to know Freddy better while riding with the Tribe and then prospecting with the Pagans. And as a new member, he was more than happy to fall in line behind him. But Glick, in many ways, was smarter than Augello. He understood the potential to make money and build status within the organization. Freddy never got that, never looked beyond or cared about anyone other than himself.

"Freddy's crime world, that's what I called it," Glick said, recounting how Augello would often use members of the club as collectors for some local mob bookmakers. Freddy claimed to have organized crime ties and was constantly touting his Sicilian heritage. He would boast about his ethnic ties to the Mafia, claiming both his father and an uncle were connected.

"Let's say a bookmaker was having trouble collecting a debt

from a customer," Glick said. "He'd call Freddy, and Freddy would send some tough-looking Pagan to talk to the deadbeat. If the guy didn't pay, Freddy'd send two or three of us to lump the guy up. After that, he usually paid. Freddy got a cut. We saw a small part of it. If Freddy got five grand, he might give us a couple of hundred each. He put the rest in his pocket. That's the way he was.

"I decided I could make more money with my own hustles, so after two or three times, I always made an excuse. I didn't want to be one of his collectors."

Glick had his day job as the executive chef at a senior citizen assisted-living facility. He was earning decent money preparing menus and arranging meals for a couple of hundred retirees. His salary was close to seventy grand. He also had a steady and ever-increasing cash stream from dealing meth and cocaine. No dummy, he had bought and sold a few properties at a profit. That was one of the reasons he was named treasurer of the club shortly after he got his colors.

"They figured I could be trusted with the money because I had plenty of my own," he said. "It just makes sense. People who have money are better treasurers than broke asses. So they gave me the books. They made me an officer, but as treasurer, you really don't have any power."

That would come later, after dozens of biker runs, a series of confrontations with the Hells Angels and other outlaw clubs and Augello's decision—brought on in part, Glick suspected, by the pill mill scam—to "retire." Freddy stepped down as president and Glick replaced him as the leader of the club early in 2012. He got the "diamond," the patch that signified he was the boss.

"In a way, Freddy was pushed out," Glick said, "although he never would admit that. There was some missing money. When we had the Roar to the Shore, we would take over a motel in Wildwood. Fill the place. The owner would charge something like two hundred twenty dollars for a room. We would have members pay us two hundred fifty dollars. The extra money, which amounted to about two thousand dollars, was to go into the club's coffers. But someone asked about this and found out there was no money. That's when Freddy stepped down. He slid over to the Atlantic County chapter and got some position with the Mother Club for a short time, just to save face. Then he retired so that no one could say he was pushed out. But everyone knew."

Augello, as a retiree, didn't have to pay club dues anymore and didn't have to go on the mandatory runs or attend the meetings. "Going to church" is the term bikers use for attending the regular weekly meetings in which business was discussed, money was collected and deals were put in place. Members were required to attend.

Glick was a different kind of president. He wasn't looking to scam other club members or to take advantage of them. He was tough. He had proven during the war with the Hells Angels that he wasn't afraid to mix it up. But he saw no need to get in anyone's face about it.

"We all have sociopathic tendencies," he said. "Being in the club brought that out in me."

But he had a natural, easy manner that put people, even hardened bikers, at ease. He had a slight stutter that was disarming and somehow added to his reputation as someone who could be trusted. By the time April Kauffman was killed, Andrew Glick was sitting atop the Cape May County chapter of the Pagans.

The first person he called after he saw the news reports about April's murder was Glenn Seeler. Seeler was the club's sergeant at arms. In the biker world, the SA is the enforcer, the go-to guy whenever there's a problem that requires muscle. Slasher, Glick knew, was one of the club members who had been approached by Augello and offered the contract to kill the doctor's wife.

"Meet me in the parking lot of the Kmart in twenty minutes" was all Glick said on the phone that afternoon. No need to say more. You never knew who might have been listening.

The Kmart was located in Somers Point, a short drive from Glick's home. He got there first and parked his pickup truck in the middle of the parking lot, away from most of the other cars. Slasher, driving his girlfriend's Mustang, pulled up almost at the same time. They got out of their vehicles and stood in the afternoon sun away from any other cars and shoppers.

"Please tell me it wasn't you," Glick said.

Slasher knew what he was talking about.

"No way," he said. "I told him I wanted no part of that. He got some fuckin' junkie to do it."

Glick was happy to hear that Slasher wasn't involved. But he was worried about the potential repercussions.

"I can't believe that motherfucker went through with this," he told Seeler. "We're all in this fucking shit."

Seeler saw it differently. He said they were just "patients" of Dr. Kauffman's.

But that was exactly the point. Glick figured investigators would start poking around Jim Kauffman's medical practice. The husband is always the first suspect when a wife is killed, and there was already plenty of talk in the social circles in which the Kauffmans moved about their troubled marriage and potential divorce. The doctor was an endocrinologist. What the hell was he doing prescribing oxycodone? And why was it that most of the patients who got those scripts were members or associates of the Pagans?

Neither Glick nor Seeler was able to contact Augello at the time of the murder. He had "gone off the grid" for a few days, Glick said. Seeler eventually made contact with him and then reported back to Glick with a message from Freddy: "Nothing's gonna come back to us. . . . It's golden. Don't worry. It's covered."

Easy to say, thought Glick, who was convinced that it wouldn't take much for law enforcement to connect the dots. "They're gonna see Pagans and a dead wife," Glick told Seeler. "And they're gonna come knocking on our doors."

That was in May 2012.

To Glick's amazement, it would be more than five years before anyone in law enforcement came knocking. He still can't believe it.

"It seemed to me, at least in the beginning, that both the doc and Freddy weren't worried about any investigation," Glick said. "It was like they knew they had someone looking out for them."

FOUR

I t was a simple condolence note.

And it changed her life forever.

Carole Weintraub, who had a successful business career but two failed marriages, would occasionally return to Absecon Island to see old friends and visit the house where she had grown up in Ventnor, a beach town just south of Atlantic City. In the spring and summer of 2012, the local newspaper, the *Press of Atlantic City*, was filled with lurid headlines about the murder of April Kauffman, the wife of her long-ago boyfriend Jimmy Kauffman.

She hadn't seen him in forty years.

"I never, ever thought in a million years that the Jimmy I knew would be involved in this," she said.

She felt she should do something. So she sent him a card. It was a condolence note from her synagogue. The note told James

Kauffman that Carole had made a donation in April's memory to a local charity.

"That's what we do," she said, explaining that it was a custom, part of her Jewish heritage. She followed up the note with a call to Jim Kauffman's office to say how sorry she was. In retrospect she will admit that the call came in part because she was curious about her old boyfriend.

"It was a polite conversation," she said. And that, she thought, was the end of it.

But Jimmy must have been curious too.

"Two or three days later, he called me and asked if I would like to meet him and go to breakfast with him," Carole recalled. "I said, sure, no problem."

There's an old Jewish joke that Carole's girlfriends told her about a bunch of Sadies clucking over a handsome new guy in the neighborhood. It's an old joke that could have served as a warning.

"Are you new around here?" one of the Sadies asked the handsome stranger. "I'm not new," he replied. "I've just been away for a while." When the women persisted in asking more questions, the handsome stranger finally told them that he had been away in jail. When they asked what for, he reluctantly admitted, "I went to jail because I killed my wife."

"Oh," said one of the Sadies, "you're a bachelor?"

Carole met Jimmy for breakfast at Caesars Atlantic City.

"It didn't take much to feel familiar again," she said. "He tried to catch me up on his life, and I did the same with my life."

Early in the conversation, she said, he told her his business had grossed more than a million dollars the previous year, an apparent attempt to impress her. Carole said she smiled and told him, "So did mine."

The conversation flowed easily from there. Carole told Jimmy about her successful business, her daughter and her unsuccessful marriages.

She had graduated from American University with a bachelor's degree in political science. Next, she went to Villanova University to earn a master's degree in history, taking summer courses from nuns who lectured in full habit. After graduate school, Carole became a headhunter. She had no business background, but discovered she was good at quickly sizing up people—a trait that seemed to fail her only when it came to choosing husbands—and matching job applicants with future employers.

"It was all baptism by fire," she said of her work as a headhunter. "It was a man's job. Many times I was the only woman at the table, and I learned a lot. I owned my own business. I had partners, but I was the one who managed the business."

Carole was a success at business, but her love life was a flop.

"My first marriage was over in the blink of an eye," she said. "It was annulled, it was that short." Her second marriage, to a general contractor, lasted sixteen years. They had one child, a daughter, but it ended badly.

"My husband decided to run off with the house painter," Carole said. The couple subsequently slugged it out through a bitter divorce.

Jim Kauffman had his own marital war stories and was happy to share them over breakfast that morning. He told Carole about his two daughters from his first marriage. Both daughters were estranged after a divorce, not only from him, Jimmy said, but also from his parents.

Carole found this upsetting. Especially the news about Jimmy's two daughters (whom she would never meet) having no relationship with their own grandmother. Carole frankly admits she had been raised in what she now realizes was a highly dysfunctional family. So she rationalized that maybe this was just the way the Kauffmans didn't work.

A couple days later, Jimmy called again and wanted to know if she would go out to dinner with him and his mother, to celebrate his mother's birthday.

She said yes.

And that was how the second act of their romance began. It was, she said, "something that was familiar and felt fine." She was proud of Jimmy for achieving the goal that he had set back in high school: to become a doctor of endocrinology. And she was impressed by the way others reacted to him.

She saw the way the guys at the garage at Caesars treated him when they went to fetch his red Corvette convertible. This was not the twenty-year-old boy she used to know, she realized. Then she saw how his patients treated him whenever they ran into him on the street, like he was God.

One day Jimmy and Carole walked into the Point Diner in Somers Point—the same diner where Joseph Mulholland had waited for Frank Mulholland on the day of the murder. In the diner, Jimmy spotted a patient of his, a big, overweight guy who was diabetic, chowing down on a tall stack of pancakes crowned with butter and syrup.

Patient and doctor locked eyes, but not a word was exchanged. Then, as Carole watched, the patient acted like "a little boy who got caught with his hand in the cookie jar" by apologizing profusely to Jimmy.

"I don't do it that often, Doc," he said. "I just wanted to treat myself."

"If you want to get better," Jimmy lectured his patient, "you can't eat like that."

When Carole asked if he was always that authoritative with patients, Jimmy said he had mellowed. In his younger days when he'd had to deal with patients who wouldn't follow his advice about cleaning up their lifestyle, he used to rip out yellow pages from the phone book that listed funeral directors and hand those pages to the disobedient patients.

"Take this, because this is the next person you're gonna have to call," he would say.

One day, he and Carole were at the beach in Longport, the posh South Jersey resort town south of Atlantic City. Carole saw Jimmy standing in the water next to an old guy of about seventy who, Jimmy had realized, was a diabetic. With that, he began lecturing the total stranger about how to take care of himself.

"Don't you want to get better?" Carole remembers him asking. When the man replied that he had kind of given up, the doctor persisted, asking, "Don't you want to have sex with your wife?"

"Oh, that ended a long time ago," the man confided while both men were standing in their wet bathing suits at the water's edge.

"I gotta leave," Carole told Jimmy. "I can't listen to this."

That was the James Kauffman who had come back into her life. She saw him as an aggressive but caring doctor who was always thinking about what was best for his patients.

"He never turned it off. . . . He was very respected."

And it seemed his patients loved him for his no-nonsense, tough-love approach. James Kauffman seemed to be the most popular endocrinologist in South Jersey.

"There were other endocrinologists, but they worked in a hospital," Carole said. In contrast, Jimmy was a single practitioner who had a "couple thousand files in the office. He had a very large practice," Carole said. He treated high cholesterol, diabetes, thyroid problems and Marfan syndrome as well as gender changes.

"Everybody went to this guy," said Amy Rosenberg, the veteran *Philadelphia Inquirer* reporter who covered the Jersey Shore. This, of course, would include members of the Pagans and their associates. But it would take a while for the authorities—and Carole—to figure out everything that was going on at James Kauffman's medical practice.

While they were dating, Carole set some ground rules. She had little interest in returning to Atlantic City, or staying at the Linwood home on the suburban, tree-lined cul-de-sac where April had been murdered. She had been in the house once or twice, she said, and "That was enough." As far as she was concerned, the place "was hideous" because it had "bad furniture, bad finishes, bad layout, tacky crap all over the place." She also considered it haunted. "But it was his house, and he loved it."

Jimmy had kept the house when his first marriage ended. He had an aviary there and an extensive garden. He raised all kinds of fruits and vegetables, which impressed Carole because it showed off Jimmy's "feminine side, the nurturing, the growing, the caring." But he was still the scientist. James Kauffman was such an expert in drip irrigation pioneered in the desert by the Israelis, a technique he used in his garden, that he would give lectures on the subject to local garden clubs.

At Carole's urging, he briefly put his house up for sale. She told him to take any offer. But when one offer finally came in and she was yelling at him, "Take it, take it," he turned it down. He didn't think the offer was good enough.

So they settled into a pattern. On Thursday nights, he would drive up to Philadelphia and stay for a long weekend at Carole's condo at the Symphony House on South Broad Street. The condo, valued at the time at nearly a million dollars, featured high ceilings, a flood of natural light, and floor-to-ceiling glass window walls twenty soaring stories above Center City Philadelphia.

Carole shared the condo with Abigail "Abby" Orobono, her daughter, who was verbally adept but developmentally disabled, and Esther, her pint-sized and pampered Brussels griffon.

At first, Jimmy didn't know if he could get along with a dog as a roommate, but Esther broke the ice by taking an immediate liking to him. He responded by being very gentle with her.

The same could not be said for the relationship between Carole's daughter, Abby, and Jim Kauffman. Abby said she had an almost toxic reaction to her mom's new boyfriend. And he apparently made little effort to change her perceptions of him.

"There was always something about him that I didn't quite like," Abby would say later. "But I did try and give him a chance for my mom's sake, but that didn't last long."

Mom and her new/old boyfriend, however, were having a great time in a new setting. The Symphony House is located on the section of South Broad Street known as the "Avenue of the Arts." It's just down the street from the Academy of Music, the oldest opera house in the country still in operation. Marian Anderson, Enrico Caruso and Edith Piaf all performed at the brick-and-brownstone concert hall that opened in 1857, as did Itzhak Perlman, Isaac Stern and Luciano Pavarotti.

The Symphony House is also just a three-block walk up the street from Philadelphia's most prestigious social club, the Union League, of which Carole was a member.

The Union League is housed in a French Empire mansion built in 1865 that occupies an entire urban block in Center City, Philadelphia. It is a private club that began during the Civil War to support both the Union and President Lincoln.

The league bills itself as a "shining jewel of history in a city defined by such treasure." Men need a sport coat and a tie to get in the front door. Dues run about $4,800 a year.

"We'd just walk right up the street and have dinner at the Union League," Carole recalled. "We had a lot of friends there."

After her divorce, dating had never worked out for Carole. Now with Jimmy, it seemed, she had finally found some happiness. Like the lyrics from that old Frank Sinatra song, love was more comfortable the second time around.

"I never met anybody that I thought was at all interesting," she said. But Jimmy "was somebody that I knew, understood and felt was in a very bad situation."

It was like taking a step back in time, rediscovering what they had had forty years earlier and let get away.

"We both were sort of on the downside of our lives, and wouldn't it be nice if we could just make the best of the time we had together?" Carole said. "We could build upon what we have now and just enjoy each other. That was our goal, and that's what we did."

They'd take trips to New York to see a Broadway show or a concert. Or fly to St. Barts for Thanksgiving.

"There wasn't a bad day," Carole recalled. "If there was something he wanted to do, I was fine with it. If there was something I wanted to do, he was fine with it."

That all this was happening within months of his wife being brutally murdered was something that Carole thought about, but was reluctant to address. The one topic they never discussed, she said, was April.

"Jimmy never really talked about her, and this was a time in our relationship where I felt that maybe it was too sensitive to talk about it," she said.

But what he would talk about was how the police were always harassing him. He said he was under constant surveillance by the cops in Jersey, who suspected him of being involved in April's murder. Police would periodically show up at his home armed with a search warrant to go through his computer, check the odometer reading on his car or confiscate his cell phone, he said.

"He had somebody constantly nipping at his heels," Carole said, estimating that the cops served Jimmy with about ten search warrants. But despite the intense scrutiny, no charges were filed. It was a game of cat and mouse that would eventually lead Jim Kauffman to the breaking point. But before that happened, he relied on his ability to compartmentalize. In his personal life, he was overjoyed about reconnecting with Carole. He responded by showering her with jewelry and exotic vacations.

But that wasn't enough.

One night before dinner at the Four Seasons Hotel in Philadelphia, a favorite haunt of theirs, they ordered drinks. A waiter in a tuxedo brought Carole a champagne glass filled with shaved ice. She noticed something else that was sparkling in the glass.

"I looked closer and saw a beautiful diamond ring that was encased in the shaved ice, and I just started to cry," Carole said.

"Part of my tears were just being overjoyed. And the other part was I wished that my mother and father were there to see this. Because they knew I had been unhappy in my previous marriage."

As a single mom, Carole had been working hard to keep her daughter, herself and her business afloat.

"I relied on myself for so long," she said. "Along comes this guy who's going to lift the load a little bit, you know. I looked at Jimmy as somebody who came along and gave me my life back. I was in such euphoria, and a little bit of sadness."

Jimmy, true to his nature, didn't seem to have any doubts.

He told Carole how overjoyed he was about how much she loved him. He talked about what a difference she had made in his life and told her he "just wanted to put a ring on it."

It was a second chance, he said, and he didn't want to let it slip by. He told her he had always regretted their breakup and wished he hadn't been that "insecure young man" who had let her walk out of his life forty years earlier.

"I think he looked at it as a continuation of where we left off when we were kids," Carole said. He told her that this time "I really want to make it work."

Like Jay Gatsby, the shady protagonist from another failed romance, Jimmy apparently believed he could repeat the past.

Carole's friends were impressed by her new boyfriend.

Michelle DuBarry was a high school classmate of Carole's; they became friends while working on the yearbook. They were an odd couple. DuBarry was a hippie who, as Miss Senior Prom, threw a tab of LSD in the punch bowl. In contrast, DuBarry remembered Carole back in high school as "super straight," somebody who "didn't smoke dope" and was "a very good girl."

Decades after high school, Michelle and Carole were still friends who made sure they got together every year to catch up. One night at dinner, after DuBarry had a couple of martinis, and while Carole was off in the ladies' room, DuBarry turned to Jim Kauffman and said, "You better not hurt her."

"Hurt her? I asked her to marry me," he replied. DuBarry said her husband, another physician, also took a liking to the new man in Carole's life.

But Carole had lingering doubts about the relationship, which she discussed with her therapist.

"Even before the engagement, I found it curious that Jimmy wanted to become involved with me as quickly as he did," she said. "I actually asked him to come with me to get my therapist's advice and opinion on it.

"The timeline didn't make sense to me," she said. April was murdered in May of 2012. Jimmy started seeing Carole in July of that same year. They were engaged by December. What Carole wanted to know was, how could he get over mourning for his murdered wife so quickly?

The cops in Jersey, of course, had their own explanation—he got over it so fast because he was responsible for the murder. But Carole saw Jimmy as innocent, a doctor who had devoted his life to healing people. She was viewing the situation through a prism that stretched back forty years. He couldn't have been a murderer. He had been her high school boyfriend; she had known him when.

The couple had one other issue, however, that was a constant flash point between them—Jimmy's harsh treatment of Carole's daughter.

"Jimmy's relationship with my daughter was terrible," Carole said. Abby has "some intellectual and emotional challenges. He [Kauffman] just couldn't abide that. He felt she was lazy and overweight and didn't do anything to take care of herself.

"He was very hard on her," she said, and he was constantly interjecting himself into mother-daughter issues. He'd "yell at her and tell her what he felt was right and wrong. I took great exception to that.

"You're not her father," Carole would tell him. "You don't have a right to tell her that. I am her mother. I will take care of that."

For her part, Abby was blunt about her feelings toward James Kauffman. In discussing all this later, she would refer to the doctor only by his surname.

"Kauffman and I had a very tumultuous and dysfunctional

relationship," she wrote in an e-mail, "meaning we didn't have one at all.

"Now that's not to say that there wasn't any sort of effort in the beginning because there was," Abby wrote about her attempts to get along with Kauffman. "My Mom can attest to that herself. But after a point I had to stop pretending that I didn't harbor any ill feelings toward Kauffman. That put a strain on my relationship with my Mom, but I knew I couldn't live a lie anymore.

"I did not trust him at all. I didn't want him around my Mom at all" because "he creeped me out. . . . He was not a nice person. . . . There was something about him that I couldn't pinpoint but I knew that he was evil."

She said that as a daughter she wanted to protect her mother. This was the case, she said, even though she knew her mom was a smart, accomplished career woman who was usually adept at sizing people up.

Abby Orobono and Kim Pack never met. Both were stepdaughters, at different times, of James Kauffman. And both came away with similar impressions of the man whom their mothers had married.

Abby conceded that "Kauffman" had treated her mother well and that her mother enjoyed the trips and the dinners and the gifts and the attention. She said her mother "did seem happy," and at the time, she was glad for that. But in an interview, Abby talked about the way he treated her when her mother wasn't there.

He was bossy, and he was nasty.

"He would make a point of telling me he didn't want me around," Abby said. And he wasn't above name-calling.

"He called me a leech. He called me a swine," Abby said. "He drove a wedge between me and my mom [because] he wanted her all to himself. He was a crazy psycho."

On a vacation Abby flew to Puerto Rico with her mother and new boyfriend. But, Abby said, it got ruined when Kauffman "jumped down my throat," telling her she shouldn't work at her high school summer camp. The doctor felt it was a waste of time for somebody like Abby, who was about to go off to college.

"I'm looking at this fool like, 'Who the hell do you think you are?'" Abby recalled. "I wanted to go home," she said. She called her father to tell him that. And when he asked why, Abby complained bitterly about her mother's new boyfriend.

"He's an ass," she told her father. At moments like that, Abby couldn't understand what her mother saw in the guy.

"She's incredibly strong and independent," Abby said. "And then he [Kauffman] rolls along and I'm like, 'What are you doing? You don't need him.'"

Her mother might have been swooning over Jimmy Kauffman, but as far as Abby was concerned, he wasn't remotely attractive. "I thought he looked like a big old gorilla," she said. "I just didn't trust him."

She also thought that he was chasing her mother "way too soon for a guy who just buried his wife." Abby's father joined the chorus of critics, telling his daughter that he was upset by the way Kauffman was treating her and less than impressed with the new man in his ex-wife's life.

"There's nothing but ice in his veins and in his eyes," Abby said her father told her.

In the midst of that personal firestorm, Carole talked Jimmy into going to see her longtime therapist, who was a psychiatrist. For James Kauffman, schmoozing Carole and her therapist was light duty. As Carole remembers it, Jimmy "put on his 'I'm the smart guy here' face and attitude and pretty much monopolized the session."

When the psychiatrist asked Jimmy about April, he replied that yes, he was still hurting over his wife's death and that he would continue to hurt. But since Carole had come into his life, he had been happy, he said. And that was why he wanted to keep Carole around. When the conversation turned to why Jimmy was being so mean to Carole's daughter, Jimmy wasn't as smooth.

He told the therapist that he thought Abby was lazy, and disrespectful to Carole. Carole responded that although this might be true, it was none of his business because he wasn't Abby's father. He responded by asking why Carole, who for the most part had raised her daughter on her own, continued to coddle her.

Even though he was a doctor, Jimmy had "very little regard for psychiatry," Carole said. He told Carole's therapist that he had patients who were more handicapped than Abby but were able to work and be productive. At the time, Abby, sick of Kauffman, was getting ready to move out of her mother's condo and head off to college. She wanted to get her own place and find a job.

During the therapy session, Carole said, "He said some awful things about Abby." The therapist was taken aback, but James Kauffman, the smartest guy in the room, "stood his ground."

Carole angrily told him that it seemed like he always needed "somebody to hate." This time it was her daughter. But once again, Jimmy wasn't going to back down. And in the end, he won.

After the session, the therapist told Carole that her worries were for naught. As far as Carole's concerns about how Jimmy was able to recover so quickly from April's murder, the therapist agreed with Jimmy. Some people take less time than others to rebound from a loss, and Jimmy must have been one of those guys. It was as simple as that.

As far as Abby was concerned, the therapist said Carole was correct: it was none of Jimmy's business. Carole's solution would be to keep the two apart as much as possible. And that would be a whole lot easier since Abby was already in the process of moving out.

And as far as Carole's relationship with Jimmy was concerned, the therapist's professional advice was "I should go on and enjoy my life," Carole said.

"Do you love each other?" the therapist asked. "Do you want to be with each other? If so, go for it."

FIVE

Jim Kauffman wanted his money. And that was what did him in.

When April Kauffman died, she had two life insurance policies. One was valued at $500,000 and the other at $100,000. Her husband was the primary beneficiary. Her daughter, Kimberly Pack, was the contingent beneficiary.

Three months after his wife's murder, Kauffman filed papers with Transamerica Life Insurance Company to collect. The insurance company balked. In June 2013, thirteen months after his wife's death, Kauffman filed suit, demanding that he be paid. In response, Transamerica, citing what is sometimes referred to as the "slayer statute," said it wouldn't pay until it was assured that "the plaintiff" (Kauffman) was not responsible for his wife's death. The insurance company wanted a police report that said as much.

By that point, police had very little traction in the murder investigation, which was more than a year old and quickly heading for a cold-case file. It was not that investigators didn't have information linking Kauffman to the murder. Mattioli had had that within three weeks of the homicide. But was it enough to take to a grand jury? Could it have resulted in an indictment and an arrest? Those are questions that continue to swirl around the case.

So while there were no formal charges related to the murder of April Kauffman, neither was there any document that would have satisfied the insurance company's request. There was nothing formally exonerating James Kauffman.

The husband is often the first suspect when a wife is murdered. Anyone involved in investigating domestic disputes—or who has watched police procedurals on television—knows that. Jim Kauffman had said as much within days of his wife's demise, so it's clear he knew that when he sought payment. Yet he pushed the issue. Maybe he thought an aggressive approach would work in his favor. Maybe he thought that if he went after the life insurance in such a public way, it would convince people that he had had nothing to do with his wife's death. Anyone who had his wife killed, he might have reasoned, would take a low profile. Surely a murderer wouldn't seek to collect $600,000 in death benefits just months after the murder was carried out. Maybe that was what he was thinking.

Or maybe he was just greedy.

Jim Kauffman never lacked for cash. He bought expensive clothes. Ate at the best restaurants. He had several cars, including a Corvette. He rode a Harley. His house in Linwood was valued at about $400,000. He had a vacation home in Tucson, Arizona. Collecting the life insurance payments would enhance his financial net worth, but he already was, on the surface at least, a wealthy man.

"Determination on the payment of death-claim benefit could not be made without first determining that plaintiff had no involvement with the death of the insured," the insurance company's lawyer wrote in response to Kauffman's lawsuit. "Transamerica therefore is unable to determine whether plaintiff may have been responsible for the intentional killing of April Kauffman."

The insurance company also noted Kimberly Pack's secondary listing in the policies and suggested she be brought into the litigation. The thirty-something daughter of April Kauffman was more than ready to engage. But not for the money, she insisted. Rather, it was a search for justice. For a year, using Facebook postings and the media, she had been keeping the memory of her mother and her murder alive. "Justice for April" was the slogan she and others had adopted in an attempt to keep public pressure on investigators and keep the murder in media news cycles.

In a "letter" to her mother that appeared in the May 2013 edition of *The Boardwalk Journal*, a monthly magazine published in Atlantic City, she described how she and her two young sons were coping with the loss one year after the fact.

"I can't begin to describe how much I miss you being part of my life," she wrote in the letter, which was spread across two pages in the magazine, the black print type imposed on a pink background. She went on to describe how her two young sons, Carter and Colton, were growing and how much they missed their grand-mother. She said her elder son, Cart, "asks about you every day and asks me if they have caught the person who has done this to you."

She wrote about her mother's gardening skills, about Thanks-giving dinner and about all she had learned from the woman she described as "my best friend, mother and sister." April Kauff-man was seventeen when she gave birth to Kim, and in many ways, they grew up together.

> *I miss meeting you for lunch, getting our hair*
> *done, going shopping, talking a million times a day,*
> *traveling together, watching my boys interacting with*
> *you, going to the makeup counter (our favorite*
> *hangout) and mostly hearing you laugh.*

Then in a more pointed reference to the tragedy and who might be responsible, she wrote:

> *You were murdered in the privacy of your own*
> *home and left for dead. It's hard to be the only*
> *family member picking up the pieces. . . . I am so sad*
> *to sit here one year later with the person responsible*
> *not brought to justice. . . . [T]he only thing I have left is*
> *hope. I have to be strong and hope that everything*
> *will work out the way it is supposed to. They say that*
> *when bad things happen and people do bad things, it*
> *catches up with them. I hope that is true and that*
> *our justice system, that is designed to protect the*
> *innocent, will triumph over evil.*

From the beginning she believed her stepfather had played a role in her mother's death. She had told Detective Mattioli that on the day of the murder and in interviews that followed. But she had not gone public with her suspicions. The letter hinted at them, but the lawsuit over the life insurance would give her and her attorney a way to say publicly what they and many others had been saying privately for more than a year. The civil litigation allowed her to publicly suggest that Jim Kauffman was a murderer.

The irony was that Kauffman had presented her with the platform.

In response to the issues raised by Transamerica in declining to pay out on the insurance policies, Kauffman's attorney, Edwin Jacobs Jr., filed papers that, among other things, contended that his client "voluntarily spoke to law enforcement in the immediate aftermath of his wife's death in an effort to assist them with their investigation." Jacobs went on to write that his client "was not involved in the death of the insured and [existing insurance law] does not require a beneficiary to affirmatively prove that he or she was not responsible for the intentional killing of the insured to collect a death benefit."

Jacobs, one of the top criminal defense attorneys in New Jersey, was hired by Jim Kauffman shortly after April Kauffman was killed. Known for his detailed analysis of cases and as a tireless courtroom advocate for his clients, the Atlantic City–based lawyer had defended some of the top organized crime figures in the Philadelphia–South Jersey area, including Philadelphia mob boss Joseph "Skinny Joey" Merlino. He had also represented onetime crime family underboss Philip "Crazy

Phil" Leonetti and been part of the defense team in the high-profile political-corruption trial of powerful Pennsylvania state senator Vincent Fumo. In dozens of battles with federal prosecutors, Jacobs had more than held his own. Kauffman's decision to hire such a well-known and highly paid defense attorney raised eyebrows in legal and law enforcement circles and reinforced the perception among some that the doctor had something to hide. If not, the theory went, why would he need the kinds of skills and expertise that Jacobs brought to the defense table? And why would he be willing to pay the hefty legal fee that secured that expertise?

In October Transamerica responded, holding to its position that it would not release the $600,000 "without first determining that plaintiff [Kauffman] had no involvement" in the murder. Then Kim Pack, through her attorney, Patrick D'Arcy, weighed in. Among other things, D'Arcy pointed out that while Jim Kauffman had, in fact, spoken to law enforcement authorities on the day his wife's body was discovered, he "had refused to answer any further questions or otherwise speak to law enforcement about the incident despite their requests."

In January 2014, at a news conference held at the firm's Egg Harbor Township offices, D'Arcy announced that he had filed papers on behalf of Kim Pack in the civil litigation. Both the lawyer and Pack emphasized that she had been pulled into the civil case by the insurance company and that she was responding to the issues. Both wanted to make it clear that Pack had not initiated any action and that her involvement was not about the money.

"Kimberly Pack . . . has been brought into the lawsuit through no fault of her own," D'Arcy said. "While we continue to undertake a massive investigation on our own, we ask that members of the Linwood community, and particularly those that knew April Kauffman, who have relevant information about the murder, to please contact us through a toll-free hotline we have set up at 844-DJD-TIPS."

Reading from a prepared statement, Kim Pack said, "I have purposely tried to avoid directly talking about what happened, but now after being brought into this lawsuit, I have no choice but to respond, and begin to fight for what I know is right. I can no longer sit back and allow what I perceive as an injustice to occur. I know that my mother would not want me to sit silently any longer."

Pack and her lawyers had been conducting their own investigation and admitted being frustrated by the apparent inaction of the Atlantic County Prosecutor's Office. "As we learned information, we turned it over to law enforcement," the law firm noted in a published synopsis of its involvement in the case, "but it seemed to fall on deaf ears."

In a wrongful-death claim filed against James Kauffman in the life insurance case, D'Arcy got quickly to the point, writing that "James Michael Kauffman is responsible for the intentional killing of April Kauffman on May 10, 2012" and that he "cannot be allowed to benefit directly or indirectly from his own wrongdoing."

It would take the Atlantic County Prosecutor's Office nearly five more years to reach that same conclusion. Kim Pack was there every step of the way. She would eventually testify about the "very rocky, very tumultuous" marriage between Jim and

April Kauffman and describe the doctor as "abusive, abrasive and narcissistic." A year before her mother was killed, Pack told investigators, her mother had wanted to end the marriage.

"She was done with him, and she wanted a divorce," she said. She went on to describe a phone call from Arizona in which her mother told Kauffman, "I hate you. I want a divorce. You're evil."

Kim Pack had already drawn that same conclusion. She talked about the paper she had written in college about Jim Kauffman's war experiences, noting that she had taped the interview for the class assignment and he later asked her to destroy the tape. His story was a combination of fact and fiction.

He said he had dropped out of college and for a time was driving a beer delivery truck. His father owned a bar in Atlantic City at the time. Kauffman had either dropped out or flunked out of Franklin & Marshall. (He was later readmitted and completed his degree.)

All of that was true.

But then he said that after dropping out he had enlisted in the Army and served in Vietnam with a Special Forces unit, surviving a jungle mission in which all the other members of his unit were killed. He enlisted for a second tour and eventually was awarded a Purple Heart.

All of that was a lie.

He had never served in the military. During a deposition taken as part of the civil litigation, he admitted as much.

With Jim Kauffman the line between fact and fiction was often blurred.

Like Kim Pack, Andrew Glick was never sure about the doctor's statements or motives.

In October of 2013, Frank Mulholland, the junkie hit man who carried out the murder of April Kauffman, was found dead in a home in the Villas, a small former fishing village in lower Cape May County. Mulholland, who was just forty-six, died of a drug overdose. Authorities found a syringe and some heroin residue in a small packet marked "Pitbull." They also found a plastic pill bottle with a prescription for oxycodone. The prescription was written by Dr. James Kauffman and filled out in the name of Joseph Mulholland. The overdose attracted very little attention outside of the pill mill underworld. This was just another drug death. Frank Mulholland, a sometime youth football and wrestling coach who had fallen on hard times, was just another victim of the opioid-heroin epidemic sweeping across America.

Or was he?

At the time of his death, no one had connected Frank Mulholland to the April Kauffman murder. Nor was there any indication that Joseph Mulholland had driven him to and from the murder scene. Later, much later, the overdose and the prescription written by James Kauffman and filled by Joe Mulholland would provide one tenuous link to the three primary players in the murder that morning back in May 2012. But no one was making those connections when Frank Mulholland was found dead.

Joseph Mulholland would later claim that he was supposed to drive into Philadelphia with Frank Mulholland on the day he overdosed. Frank Mulholland never showed up, and later in the day, Joseph Mulholland and a friend went to his home in the Villas. When Frank Mulholland didn't respond to a knock on the door, they looked through a window and saw him sprawled on the floor. They immediately called 911. Joseph Mulholland said he had lived briefly with Frank Mulholland, and that was why the plastic prescription container with his name on it was found on the premises. He said he had given Frank Mulholland the pills in lieu of paying rent for the brief time he lived with him. Joe Mulholland denied he had had anything to do with Frank Mulholland's death and said he had warned Frank to "stay away" from Augello. Augello, he said, had talked about "taking out" Frank, fearing that "the junkie" might confess to authorities about the murder if he were confronted.

Joseph Mulholland, one of several members of the pill mill ring who would eventually cooperate with authorities, said he had served as the getaway driver in the murder of April Kauffman out of fear.

"Fred told me if I didn't do it, I would be next," he said.

For James Kauffman and Fred Augello, Frank Mulholland's death tied up one loose end in the murder case. Andrew Glick, who wasn't privy to the details, was one of the first to put the pieces together. What he learned, from bits of information and direct and indirect comments from the doctor and the Pagan biker boss, was that Frank Mulholland had been raising a stink about the money he had received for killing April Kauffman. He thought he should have been paid more.

Whether he knew that the doctor had put up $50,000 for the hit is open to speculation. But what seems certain is that he felt the $10,000 he was paid by Augello wasn't enough. Freddy had apparently tried to placate Mulholland by making him an "honorary" member of the Pagans, Glick said. There was, of course, no such title in the biker underworld. Augello had also designed a fancy stick for Mulholland. The wooden club had the words "Ice Man" and "Pagans Forever" and the letters "LPDP" (Live a Pagan, Die a Pagan) carved artistically along its sides. "Ice Man" was an apparent attempt by Augello to play on Mulholland's ego. There was a notorious underworld hit man from North Jersey, Richard Kuklinski, who was known as the Iceman. He was convicted of murdering six people but was believed to have been involved in at least a dozen more homicides. Most were contract killings, some carried out for underworld figures. Frank Mulholland was Freddy Augello's Ice Man, Glick said.

Police responding to the Mulholland overdose gathered up the drug paraphernalia, the plastic prescription container and other pieces of evidence tied to the death. They also seized the decorative wooden club. Glick said the carvings were an example of Augello's talent as an artist.

"Freddy could draw anything," Glick said.

But artistry doesn't pay the bills.

In the summer of 2013, a few months before he turned up dead, Frank Mulholland had shown up at Augello's sign company off Route 9. Glick and several other bikers were there, hanging out, preparing to make a bike run.

"I remember it was a nice day, warm, a good day for a ride," he said. "There were four or five of us there and this guy bebops in driving a beat-up pickup truck. He and Freddy have a conversation, and then I hear Freddy say to him, 'Give me a moment.' Then he walks over to Slasher, who was the sergeant at arms, and tells him and this other guy who we called Rehab to 'get this guy out of here. He's a real knucklehead.'"

Glick said he watched as Rehab and Slasher walked Frank Mulholland back toward his pickup truck. Suddenly Rehab started to pound him. He and Slasher "lumped him up," Glick said. Mulholland, bruised and bloody, was told, "Don't ever come back." He got into his pickup truck and drove away. Glick didn't think very much about it. At the time, he had no idea who Frank Mulholland was or what role he had played in the April Kauffman murder. This was just a guy who had a beef with Freddy, and this was the way Freddy dealt with it. The guy got "lumped up." Nobody asked why. That was the way of the world when you were a Pagan. Besides, it was a perfect day for a ride, and a few minutes after Mulholland was beaten, the bikers were on the road, heading south toward a bar where there would be booze and maybe some broads.

It was good to be a Pagan, Glick thought.

Glick learned that after the confrontation with Augello, Frank Mulholland arrived one day unannounced at Kauffman's medical office and demanded money. The doctor apparently claimed not to know what Mulholland was talking about. This was around the same time Kauffman had opened his legal dispute over the $600,000 in life insurance. The irony was not lost on Glick when he learned later how all the pieces fit. Here was the hit man, in the doctor's office, making the same type of claim that Kauffman was making in court, looking for a bigger payout, claiming he was entitled.

How and why Frank Mulholland died are two intriguing questions that continue to hover over the April Kauffman murder case. Did he die of an overdose? Or did someone kill him? The Cape May County Prosecutor's Office, which originally listed the death as an overdose, reopened the case in 2019 as a possible murder.

Augello would eventually be convicted for setting the April Kauffman hit in motion, for hiring Frank Mulholland and for collecting the cash offered by James Kauffman. He continues to deny those charges. At his sentencing hearing in December 2018, Augello claimed he didn't know Frank Mulholland and never hired him to kill April. Instead, he claimed Joseph "Irish" Mulholland told him that he had arranged a heroin "hot shot" that caused Frank Mulholland's death. Joseph Mulholland has told authorities there is no truth to that allegation.

One final irony. The nurse practitioner who worked in Jim Kauffman's office, the woman who shortly after the murder had told authorities about Kauffman's "biker patients," was the medical official called in to pronounce Frank Mulholland dead of the drug overdose in the home where his body was found.

Mulholland died in October of 2013. Glick remembers visiting the doctor's office that month and being somewhat confused by something Jim Kauffman told him.

"I took care of that junkie," he said Kauffman told him. "You don't have to worry about it no more."

"Good for you," Glick said he responded, pretending to understand. But he was actually in the dark. Later he heard that Mulholland was dead, but initially thought it was Joseph "Irish" Mulholland.

"I went to see Freddy, and I said, 'Irish is dead?'" Glick recalled. "Freddy told me it wasn't Irish. It was his cousin. I didn't know who that was."

Augello, he said, told him it was the knucklehead who had

shown up that day at the sign shop, the guy who got tuned up by Slasher and Rehab. Then, Glick said, Augello told him that Frank Mulholland was the hit man in the April Kauffman murder. "He looked at me, made the sign of a gun with his fingers and said, 'He was the guy who did this.'"

That was when Glick said he first learned who had carried out the hit. And that's when he put all the pieces together.

In many ways Frank Mulholland was the second victim in a murder case that sent shock waves through Atlantic County. But at the time, his death had very little impact on the murder investigation. No one in law enforcement had any information that would link the junkie to the murder.

There was, however, one person who knew, or at least suspected, Frank Mulholland had killed April Kauffman.

Mulholland's nephew Tim Sarzynski would later testify that his uncle told him in the summer of 2012 that he was the shooter. They were on a fishing trip, Sarzynski said, and had stopped at a Wawa to buy something to eat. There was a magazine rack and one of the magazines had a story about the April Kauffman murder.

Mulholland pointed to the magazine, his nephew said, and told him, "I did that."

Sarzynski said he didn't know what to think. He said that his uncle had a tendency to exaggerate, that he had a loose affiliation with the truth. Later, when the case unfolded, he came forward and told authorities about that day and what his uncle had told him.

"He told me he walked into her bedroom, shot her twice in the back of the head and said he was paid fifty thousand dollars," the nephew said from the witness stand at Fred Augello's trial. The story, at best, is fraught with inconsistencies. But then, as Sarzynski said, "My uncle often made up stories."

There was a consistency, however, in Frank Mulholland's less-than-factual account. Joe "Irish" Mulholland said Frank told him on the day of the murder that he had shot April Kauffman twice in the back of the head. April Kauffman had been shot twice, but not in the back of the head.

There was also a crime scene ballistic report indicating that a bullet was found in the bedroom wall and another in the bedsheets. Were there more than two shots fired that morning? And was there more than one shooter?

Finally, there was this. While the official time of death based on at least two medical examiner reports was around five thirty a.m., a third medical examiner briefly involved in the case placed the time of death at around two a.m.

Was April Kauffman already dead when Frank Mulholland entered the bedroom?

Frank Mulholland might have provided answers to several questions that still hover over the case, had he not died of a drug overdose. Maybe he knew too much. Maybe he had learned that Dr. Kauffman had put a $50,000 contract out on his wife. Maybe that was why he confronted Augello and then the doctor about more money.

And maybe that was why he was dead.

Glick wasn't sure what to make of all the information he accumulated in the summer and fall of 2013. He was still perplexed, as well, by the fact that law enforcement hadn't put any of the pieces together. There were rumors floating around the underworld of a possible Pagans involvement in the murder. And anyone with access to Jim Kauffman's patient list would readily see a half dozen members of the biker club or their close associates listed as patients who were regularly receiving scripts for oxycodone.

"He had to have somebody looking out for him," Glick said of Dr. Kauffman. "Someone holding that umbrella. None of this was going to fall on him. Somebody in politics or government who didn't want all the details about the Kauffmans and their swinging lifestyle to come out. Maybe somebody who was swinging with them. That's the only thing that would make sense."

Glick did have to answer to a higher authority, however. In the fall, around the same time that Frank Mulholland turned up dead, Glick was called on the carpet by three leaders of the Pagans Mother Club from North Jersey.

"This would have been around October," Glick said. "They came down to my house. I was living off Zion Road in North-field at the time. That's where we used to have our meetings. It was me, Slasher and a couple of other members of our chapter. This guy Jersey Jim came down from the Mother Club, asking about some talk they were hearing on the grapevine about somebody connected with the Atlantic County or Cape May County chapter of the Pagans being involved in the murder of this woman April Kauffman."

Glick told the head of the New Jersey chapter of the Pagans that he didn't know anything about it.

"I lied to his face," he said. "But I told him we'd keep our eyes and ears open and let him know if we heard anything. If we took a murder contract, the Mother Club would have wanted to know.

Plus they would have wanted a piece of the payout. It was the same thing with the pill mill. Freddy never told them about that, or he would have had to kick some money up to them. He wasn't about to do that. So I just denied knowing anything about the murder and didn't say a word about the oxycodone scripts the doc was writing for us."

Like law enforcement, Glick said, the Mother Club didn't appear interested in pursuing the matter any further. He began to think that it might have been possible for the doc and Freddy Augello to get away with murder. Neither seemed concerned about being held accountable. Freddy had more money than he had ever had. And the doc was living the life of a wealthy and well-connected endocrinologist. The civil litigation over the life insurance policy was something he had to deal with, but the potential payout was apparently worth the aggravation. He wasn't looking back but rather looking ahead.

On August 31, 2013, just fifteen months after April Kauffman was murdered, Jim Kauffman married his high school sweetheart, Carole Weintraub.

SIX

The bride wore a summer frock and a short cardigan sweater to cover her bare arms, out of respect for the historic synagogue they were standing in. The groom wore a suit and tie.

Carole and Abby, her attendant, carried bouquets of flowers that Jim Kauffman gave them. An old friend was his attendant. The wedding took place in Rodeph Shalom, Carole's synagogue. Founded in 1795, it's the oldest Ashkenazic synagogue in the entire western hemisphere. The reform congregation is housed in a distinctive 1927 Moorish Revival–style temple on North Broad Street in North Philadelphia. It's a historic landmark with a limestone front, intricate tile work and columns and a lavish interior filled with mosaics, marble floors and stained glass windows.

The ceremony, conducted by Carole's rabbi, didn't last ten minutes.

"We don't go in for a lot of glitz and glamour," Carole said. Because it was the third marriage for both of them, "it was very low-key." She didn't even buy a new dress.

But, Carole said, it was lovely.

"I cried through the entire ceremony," she said. "I really missed my father and so wanted him to be there."

Carole's daughter, Abby, also felt deep emotions. But of a different sort.

"I was gritting my teeth the entire time," she said. She even forced herself to smile for pictures. "I played the dutiful daughter. I just pretended to be happy for her."

From the synagogue, they went to the Four Seasons for a quiet dinner celebration. They left the next day on a cruise to Europe. They spent nine days visiting Guernsey and Dover, an English seaside town where they rode bicycles. Then they visited the Bordeaux wine country in France before going on to Spain, to see Seville and Barcelona.

When they came back from their honeymoon, the couple settled into "an easy, relaxed life," Carole said. "It was like we had picked up where we left off as kids. We felt lucky enough to be able to reconnect, and we tried to make the most of what we had."

Both wondered about what might have been had they stayed together forty years earlier.

"We were virtually the same person," Carole said of that relationship so long ago. Jimmy Kauffman, she said, was her first love. They were a couple of blue-collar Jewish kids who grew up in the 1960s a mile away from each other on Absecon Island. That's the eight-mile-long barrier island off the southern coast of New Jersey that includes Atlantic City, Ventnor, Margate and Longport.

Atlantic City was always the hub around which everything revolved. It was a city built on dreams that never seemed to come true and promises that were seldom kept. It was a giant carnival act that offered tourists the sizzle but not the steak. It was a city driven by greed and incompetence, vice and corruption.

Carole and Jimmy grew up decades after the Boardwalk Empire days of Enoch "Nucky" Johnson, the corrupt politico who ruled the island and oversaw the distribution of shipments of bootleg liquor that seemed to wash up with the tide.

"In Atlantic City," a local wag once opined, "Prohibition was merely a suggestion."

And Carole and Jimmy had both left the area before gambling was legalized on the boardwalk and another amoral rogue, a future president named Donald Trump, would come to town to slap his name on several brand-new casino-hotels.

Johnson, the inspiration for the HBO series *Boardwalk Empire*, was the Atlantic County sheriff and political boss who got a piece of all the illegal action flourishing in the speakeasies and brothels of the city then known as the "World's Playground."

"We have whiskey, wine, women, song and slot machines," the *New York Times* quoted Johnson as saying. "I won't deny it, and I won't apologize for it. If the majority of the people didn't want them, they wouldn't be profitable, and they wouldn't exist. The fact that they do exist proves to me that the people want them."

At the height of his power, Nucky lived in a suite of rooms that took up the entire ninth floor of the Ritz-Carlton Hotel on the boardwalk. He wore a raccoon coat, had a fresh red carnation pinned every day to the lapel of his expensive suit and was chauffeured around town in a twelve-cylinder powder blue Rolls-Royce Silver Ghost limo.

But by the time Carole and Jimmy were coming of age, Nucky was dead. And so was the era in which he had flourished. The glamour of the former Boardwalk Empire had faded into a seedy tourist trap. The regulars who were stuck living year-round on the island during an economic downturn were left only with memories of past glory.

"People would talk about the old days, when women would stroll the boardwalk in fur stoles and high heels, men were in jackets and ties with big cigars," Carole said. The old-timers reminisced about what used to be Atlantic City's calling cards: white sand beaches and big beautiful old hotels. But the beaches eroded, and the old hotels were torn down, replaced by empty lots, cheap souvenir shops and auction houses that sold imitation goods at grossly inflated prices to gullible tourists.

If New York is the Big Apple and New Orleans is the Big Easy, then Atlantic City was, and remains, the Big Hustle. Everyone was looking for a score.

Carole's and Jimmy's families had a lot in common. Their fathers were a couple of battle-scarred World War II vets who owned struggling bars. Once, drunken conventioneers on holiday used to pack the local watering holes and direct unwanted attention to young women like Carole. But in the 1960s, conventioneers abandoned Atlantic City for cheap and plentiful flights to Las Vegas, America's more popular adult playground.

As a result, both Carole's and Jimmy's mothers were forced to work odd jobs to supplement losses to the family income.

"We lived in the same style house," Carole recalled, a couple of one-story bungalows with three bedrooms and "a living room decorated for show but never used."

The Weintraubs were on the one hundred block of North Swarthmore Avenue in Ventnor City; the Kauffmans on the one hundred block of North Gladstone Avenue in Margate.

Carole's house had all-white aluminum siding and a porch under an awning, where she could sit outside and stay dry on rainy days. The neighborhood was largely poor and Jewish. Carole had an older brother who was off on his own most of the time. He left home as soon as he could.

"I didn't know we were schleppers," Carole said. She remembers walking home from school and passing Mrs. Cohen's house next door, where she would be engulfed by the aroma of homemade chicken soup.

"Gee, that smells nice, Mrs. Cohen," Carole would say. And Mrs. Cohen would invite Carole in for a bowl.

Jimmy, an only child, was always interested in science, and Carole was impressed when his parents bought him a chemistry set. He set up a lab in the garage, which his father, who made furniture, had converted into a workshop. Carole can still remember him peering through his microscope, conducting experiments and dissecting animals.

But while the Weintraubs and the Kauffmans were attractive and industrious on the exterior, behind closed doors both families suffered from similar problems.

"We came from physically abusive, very dysfunctional families," Carole said. Jimmy's father was "a very angry man" who saw his chances of success disappear when he wasn't able to fulfill his dream of going to West Point. Instead, he went to war and wound up cutting pilots and gunners out of trees on Omaha Beach.

"My mother was the female version, an extremely angry woman who thought my father was going to be the ticket to an affluent life," Carole said. Instead, her parents wound up struggling to make ends meet.

Both families were profoundly impacted by World War II.

Jimmy's mother, Ruth Kempner, was born and raised in Berlin, Germany. She was fortunate to escape capture by the Nazis, who were rounding up Jews after *Kristallnacht* (the Night of Broken Glass) in 1938. She owed her life to a British rescue operation known as the *Kindertransport*, a volunteer program in which the British government allowed unaccompanied children from Germany and Eastern Europe to enter the country on temporary visas. The program depended on private citizens and volunteer organizations to pay for each child's care and education.

From 1938 to 1940, according to the United States Holocaust Memorial Museum, the program saved nearly ten thousand predominantly Jewish kids. But more than 1.5 million children would die in the concentration camps. Jimmy's mother was one of the lucky ones. She met her husband at a dance in London sponsored by local Jewish charities. At the time, Jack Kauffman was recovering from war wounds. They got married in London, before moving to the States.

They made a handsome couple. Jack Kauffman had a sculpted face and deep dimples that won him a job after the war modeling tuxedos for After Six, a men's clothing manufacturer based in Philadelphia. Ruth, slim and petite, was never seen with a hair out of place. The couple shared their home with Ruth's German mother.

Carole's parents grew up in Philadelphia, before moving to Absecon Island. Her father, Irwin Weintraub, dubbed "Elchick" in Yiddish, was the dapper son of a former bootlegger. As a senior at Temple University, Elchick was known for his fancy clothes, strawberry blond hair and blue eyes. He took Carole's mother, a striking woman, to Temple's senior prom in a brand-new Ford convertible.

Five months later, the Japanese bombed Pearl Harbor. Elchick signed up for ROTC and became an Army officer, supervising the construction of airstrips in preparation for D-Day. He would not see his new bride for almost five years.

When they came home from the war, both fathers coped with trauma but couldn't verbalize their problems. Instead, they adopted the roles dictated by the sexual standards of the time. Men had to be strong and silent.

"Both homes were filled with secrets," Carole said. "Our dads never talked about their war experiences. We inherently knew that the war discussion was verboten."

Carole's mother, named Fanny Kazinetz at birth, changed her name to Frances. She was a lifelong tomboy and jock the neighbors called "Fency," another Yiddish nickname. As a kid, Fency was so tough she would beat up boys. As an adult, she was such a competitor that she would play stickball with the boys on her street. But when she cleaned up, Fency was quite a looker.

Friends who visited Carole at her house would stare at her mother's framed photo and say, "Who's the movie star?"

"Movie star? That's my mother," Carole would respond. Her friends thought that when she dressed up, Fency looked like Hedy Lamarr or Sophia Loren. But Fency had a dark side; she was prone to violence and was physically abusive with her daughter.

"She hit me. She locked me in a closet. She would slap me around," Carole said. She couldn't depend on her dad to protect her. "My father worked all the time," Carole said.

Even when he was around, nothing changed in the violent mother-daughter dynamic.

"In those days, dads were just hands off," Carole said.

Jimmy, Carole would subsequently learn, had suffered similar abuse at the hands of his father; so the two had that sad dysfunction in common.

For Carole and Jimmy, getting an education at Atlantic City High School during the 1960s was a challenge.

"We went to the same high school, a run-down old building where parts of the basement were condemned, some of the windows worked, and [only] some of the teachers cared," Carole said. "It was a strange mix of students since there was only one high school on the island.

"The down-beach kids were white, some very prosperous. Many families owning businesses were able to provide for their children and give them a reasonable chance of doing better and achieving more than they did."

The uptown students were mostly black and poor, some of whom got their only meal of the day at school. Academically, the uptown students were pushed through, whether they were up to par or not, so there would be enough room for the next class.

Racial tensions typically ran high.

"All it took was for someone to throw a stool in the cafeteria or stab someone with a fork, and a racial riot would ensue," Carole recalled.

In contrast to many of their peers, Carole and Jimmy were both serious students. "We weren't the popular kids, but rather individuals that didn't fit anywhere," she said. Most of her class-mates "were pretty immature" and interested in things that seemed trivial to Carole, such as who had the best clothes and who was going out with whom on Saturday night.

It was easy for Carole and Jimmy to stay practical because they both had to work odd jobs to support themselves through high school. They weren't hippies, so they had no interest in the marijuana and LSD that were popular with their classmates. After school and on the weekends, Carole worked as a waitress at Howard Johnson's and at local diners, including a little fam-ily restaurant around the corner from her house.

The owner would pick up Carole, wearing her waitress uni-form, in his station wagon on the way to setting up for the breakfast shift. But before they got to the restaurant, they had to stop at the dump and drop off the previous day's garbage.

"The garbage and I were in the backseat," Carole remem-bered.

Jimmy, who graduated from high school three years before

she did, was enrolled in college and during the summers worked as a Teamster driving a beer truck, delivering Ballantine Ale and Colt 45 malt liquor to bars and restaurants.

"We did what we needed to do to survive," Carole said. They were waiting for the day "when we could leave home and begin to reinvent ourselves."

Their first date was set up by friends.

At five feet nine, James Michael Kauffman was an athlete who had played baseball and racquetball in high school. He was an upperclassman whom she had admired from afar. He had dark hair, light brown eyes and a "beautiful smile," Carole recalled. "He was a very good-looking guy," a younger version of his father, the former tuxedo model.

"I can still see him standing in my living room in Ventnor, wearing a maroon sport coat and nice trousers and a kerchief around his neck," Carole said. "He thought he was just the stud of the earth. His shoes were shined; I even think he had a pocket square."

Carole Lee Weintraub was just seventeen.

On their first date, Carole wore a sweater and a skirt, knee socks and Weejuns. She was five feet two with a knockout figure, dark eyes and dark hair down to her waist. People thought she looked Israeli or Middle Eastern.

Jimmy was very old-school smooth with Carole's parents, shaking her father's hand and making polite conversation. He came across as quite the catch, a college man three years older than Carole, and a premed student to boot at Franklin & Marshall College in Lancaster, Pennsylvania.

"I envied him [because] he knew at a young age that he

wanted to be a doctor, every Jewish mother's dream," Carole said.

But it wasn't love at first sight.

"We had one date, and I think he ran for the hills," Carole said. They went out for dinner at a long-forgotten restaurant. "I think he was happy when he dropped me at the door," Carole said. "I think I was happy when he left."

Later that year, however, Carole found herself in a predicament, as a senior with no date for the prom or graduation. Out of desperation, she asked Jimmy to be her prom date, "never thinking he would say yes.

"He agreed to accompany me, and from that point on, we were inseparable," she said.

The romance, which officially began in June 1970, was easy because the two had so much in common. Besides attending the same high school, they went to the same Orthodox synagogue where the men met downstairs for the minyan, and the women had to sit in upstairs in the balcony. "We were so comfortable with each other," Carole said. "It was almost like there was no learning curve."

But Jimmy wasn't like the other kids. When he had walked the halls in high school, when he was a senior and Carole was a freshman, he hadn't paid attention to anybody. He had always seemed preoccupied.

"He looked like the kind of guy whose mind was somewhere else," Carole remembered. "He had his future mapped out. I would consider him an out-of-the-box thinker. He came at issues and events from a different perspective than most people did. . . . He was always ten steps ahead of everybody else."

Even then he thought of himself as the smartest guy in the room.

But Carole subsequently discovered that he had a tender, nurturing side. It showed when she was seriously injured in an accident.

The day before high school let out, Carole went to a local burger joint to get something for lunch. While in the restaurant, she thought she caught a glimpse of Jimmy's beer truck whizzing by the window. She turned quickly to her right and wound up crashing through a glass wall.

Carole was in shock and covered with blood; a girlfriend called an ambulance. She needed more than a hundred stitches and was out of commission for six weeks.

"I was bandaged all the way up to my thigh," Carole said. Her arms were bandaged too.

Some boyfriends might have moved on, but Jimmy stopped by every day for six weeks to help care for Carole. He was so attentive he even washed her waist-length hair in a laundry basin. That got to Carole, who recalled, "I was so in love."

Another reason Carole fell for Jimmy: he stood up to her mother, which nobody else had done before.

For example, after high school, Carole got accepted at American University in Washington, DC.

Before she left for school, Carole was going out to buy bathroom supplies at the drugstore: soap, shampoo, conditioner, et cetera. Her mother handed Carole a ten-dollar bill, which didn't fly with Jimmy. He looked at the ten-dollar bill and told her mother, "What's she going to do with that? That's not enough."

Carole was stunned. "What you have to understand," she said, was that "nobody crossed my mother."

As Carole watched, her chagrined mother asked Jimmy how much money she should give Carole. He said twenty dollars, and then Carole's mother handed her a twenty-dollar bill.

Jimmy also used to tease Carole's mother about the instant coffee she served. "That's not coffee," he would say to her. Carole's mother had no response.

"I think she was a little afraid of him," Carole said.

After Carole went off to school, Jimmy, who had dropped out of college when his grades plummeted, returned to Franklin & Marshall to continue his premed studies.

"We saw each other every other week," alternating between college towns, Carole said. He had an apartment in Lancaster not far from campus. Rent was sixty dollars a month, and the gas bill was about eight dollars.

When Carole visited Lancaster, the couple would go to movies or visit the farms and farmers markets in Pennsylvania Dutch Country. They'd hit the pretzel factory, where they would buy broken pretzels for a dollar. When they had enough cash, which Jimmy would always count out on a table beforehand, "we would treat ourselves to a nice dinner," Carole said.

There was more to do in Washington, plenty of museums to visit and concerts to attend.

"It was wonderful," Carole recalled. "We were in love and very devoted to each other."

They'd go out for a drive in Jimmy's turquoise 1968 Chevy Impala, a gift from his aunt. When the Carpenters' "Close to

You" played on the radio, Carole and Jimmy would sing along. At first, that was how happy they were.

During the summer, they spent their rare days off at the Swarthmore Avenue beach, after Carole swapped her ketchup-covered waitress uniform for a two-piece bathing suit. "We both loved the ocean," she said. The soundtrack to their romance was provided by Crosby, Stills & Nash; Santana; James Taylor; and Carole King.

"We had a great time," Jimmy wrote Carole in a note after a 1970 date. "I want you to know that I love you and that you are the nicest girl. I wish I could be there to keep you warm."

Some of his actions, however, had begun to put a chill on the romance. Over time Carole discovered Jimmy Kauffman had "some flaws in his personality that began to bother me."

It started with an argument over a piece of jewelry.

"He became extremely possessive, insisting that I wear his college pin all the time," Carole said. When she refused, he became incensed.

"I guess he needed that visual confirmation that I didn't think was that important," Carole said.

Carole noticed other problems.

"He was jealous of the time I spent with family and friends. I had to tell him where I was whenever we were apart."

As a kid with a volatile, abusive mother and a passive father who functioned as his wife's enabler, Carole had gotten used to being on her own, to finding her own way. She remembered feeling that way as an eight-year-old in second grade. Now, when she was a college student, her independent streak had only grown stronger. Her relationship with Jimmy, she decided, had become too confining.

"For someone like me who valued independence, well, it was just overwhelming, and I had this feeling of being smothered," she said. "We were never with his friends. It had to be just us all the time."

She made up her mind that she had to end it. They were in Jimmy's apartment when Carole broke the bad news. "I can't do this anymore," she told him. "I want to go my own way."

Jimmy, she said, went to pieces.

"He literally got down on his hands and knees and cried and pleaded with me not to leave," Carole said. "He begged me to stay and told me he would change."

Some women might have been flattered, but Carole was upset.

"It made me sick," she recalled. "I thought it was horrifying and sad, and it scared me. I thought, this is not a rational response. This is so desperate and horrible that there must be something wrong with him. I thought he was sick and not in control of himself."

She reluctantly agreed to stay.

"Being nineteen and pretty naïve about human nature, I agreed," she said. "So I left, got on the bus and went back to school. But it didn't take long to understand that he couldn't change."

The very next weekend, Carole came back. When he acted like the same old Jimmy, she told him again, "I can't do this anymore."

This time, Jimmy's reaction was completely different.

"He got very angry with me," she said.

"Just get out," he told her. "Just leave." His attitude, Carole said, was "good riddance to bad rubbish."

Carole got on the bus and went back to Washington.

This time for good.

And so the romance ended after two years in the summer of 1972.

"He was my first boyfriend," she said. "He loved me. He cared about me. It was more than I ever got from anybody. In the house that I grew up in, I thought I was unlovable."

Her grandfather told her she was crazy for breaking up.

"What do you mean, you couldn't get along with him?" he asked. "What difference does that make? He's gonna be a doctor."

But Carole had made up her mind; the breakup was final.

"There was no going back. I couldn't be with him . . . until we reconnected forty years later."

A few months after the honeymoon, they hosted a small reception at the Union League for friends and family members. There were about a hundred guests there to greet them and celebrate a marriage that both agreed was forty years overdue.

"I got up to thank everybody for coming," Carole said. "Then I told a couple of funny stories."

When it was Jimmy's turn to speak, he couldn't.

Carole watched in shock as he "just broke down and started to cry like a baby."

It was a happy, festive occasion tinged with a touch of sadness about those who couldn't be there, of parents who had passed away, of old memories the couple shared and thoughts of what might have been if only they had stayed connected.

Some of the guests at the Union League wedding reception knew the history, the backstory. Many were happy that Carole and Jimmy had gotten back together, rekindling a romance that was, indeed, better the second time around.

But not everybody shared the newlyweds' happiness. Carole's daughter, Abby, had plenty of doubts about where this romance was going. To Abby, Kauffman was an overly possessive guy who had stalked her mother for forty years in his hunt for a "trophy wife."

Shortly after the wedding and long before the reception at the Union League, Abby had experienced some nasty residual effects from the marriage. When word got out on Facebook about James Kauffman remarrying so soon after April's murder, she began receiving unwanted messages on her Facebook page from a woman who claimed to be one of April's friends.

The woman told Abby to keep an eye on her new "step-daddy," and advised her to sleep with a knife under her pillow. She also wrote that her mother deserved to die because she was hanging out with a man who had just murdered his wife.

Abby showed the messages to both Kauffman and her mother. Carole was horrified and proceeded to block the woman from Abby's Facebook page. It was an ugly distraction during what was by and large a happy time for the new couple. The newlyweds enjoyed living in the moment and talking about their future together. Jimmy had his second home in Tucson, Arizona, which he loved. He was considering cutting back his workload in Jersey and eventually retiring in Arizona.

Carole, however, hated the desert. "It's hot, it's flat, it's brown," she said. "There's no water there."

She was also concerned about Jimmy's finances.

"He wasn't as financially secure as I originally thought," she said. "There were some things that I couldn't understand about his finances."

While he had a successful medical practice, generating more than a million dollars a year in revenue, he was in arrears on his taxes and had taken out some loans on his house in Jersey. He explained to Carole "that there was a tremendous amount of spending that went on in his marriage. He didn't want to declare bankruptcy. He was trying to dig himself out of a hole," she said.

But they disagreed about how to handle the debt.

"He was drilling down on his payments, but not fast enough as far as I was concerned," Carole said. She thought he should have been putting more money down on his debts.

"If you have debts, let's get rid of the debt," Carole argued. But according to Carole, Jimmy replied, "No, let's pay the minimum. Let them wait for their money. I want to enjoy my life."

To help straighten out his business life, Carole went to work for about nine months as a consultant for her husband, doing some human resources work, soliciting résumés, interviewing job candidates and helping him get updated with employment practices and employment law.

For a guy deep in debt, however, James Kauffman always had a lot of cash around. He usually paid for dinners at restaurants by whipping out a hefty bankroll. He explained his ever-present stash of cash to Carole by saying that in his building there was a blood lab that was a tenant of his and paid the rent in cash. In the practice of endocrinology, everything is built around blood tests, he told Carole. The lab paid him more than $10,000 every month for rent, something he didn't want to advertise.

"It wasn't against the law, but it was frowned upon to have a relationship with a laboratory in his medical office," Carole said her new husband told her.

As authorities would subsequently discover, however, the lab was routinely overbilling Medicare for unnecessary blood work done on Jimmy's patients. Whether Dr. Kauffman knew what was going on with the scam was another mystery. As far as the authorities were concerned, James Kauffman's arrangement with the blood lab wasn't the only ethical line that he was willing to cross. They were also curious about all the oxycodone prescriptions he was writing for members of the Pagans and their associates.

SEVEN

The numbers are staggering . . . and ever growing.

The National Institute on Drug Abuse estimates that more than 115 people die every day in the United States from overdosing on opioids.

Every day.

And if that tragic statistic isn't enough, consider the economic burden of the drug crisis. Studies have indicated that the costs tied to medical services, rehab programs, job loss and law enforcement efforts are $78.5 billion annually. In that light, the pill mill operation at the center of April Kauffman's murder seems almost inconsequential.

But the murder offers a look inside the opioid crisis and an explanation for how drugs like oxycodone—a drug that pharmaceutical firms had initially claimed was not addictive—make their way to the streets.

Phony prescriptions written by unscrupulous doctors who have forgotten or chosen to ignore the ethics of their profession are the primary source of the drugs. Networks of drug dealers using teams of bogus patients to secure the scripts are step two. Pharmacists willing to fill those phony scripts are the third crucial part of the process.

In the end, the pills, usually paid for by unsuspecting insurance companies, are sold on the streets for twenty to thirty dollars apiece. A one-month prescription for sixty pills has a street value of up to $1,800. A pill mill operation with just ten "patients" would generate $18,000 a month, or $216,000 a year.

Every day, it seems, law enforcement authorities are announcing arrests tied to lucrative pill mill operations. In February 2018 ten doctors were charged in Virginia and West Virginia with flooding the market with oxycodone and causing the deaths of at least two of their patients. In announcing arrests that capped a four-year investigation, a federal prosecutor described the physicians charged in the case as "drug dealers hidden behind the veil of a doctor's lab coat, a medical degree and a prescription pad."

In May five doctors in the Pittsburgh area were charged with running a pill mill out of several addiction clinics, leading one newspaper to top an opinion piece about the arrests with the headline "Doctors That Run 'Pill Mills' Deserve the Same Punishment as Crack Dealers."

And in October federal authorities in New York announced the arrests of five doctors charged with "taking millions of dollars in return for prescribing oxycodone pills to purported patients with no legitimate medical need for them," according to a *New York Times* report. Several patients, including two employees in one of the doctors' offices, died from drug overdoses. One of the doctors charged in the case ran a medical clinic in Queens where he wrote scripts for 3.3 million pills paid for by Medicare and Medicaid, the newspaper reported.

"Instead of caring for their patients, these doctors were drug dealers in white coats," said a federal prosecutor.

Jim Kauffman wore one of those coats, hiding behind it while he wrote scripts for both oxycodone and compound pain cream—scripts that netted him tens of thousands of dollars per month in schemes that contributed to the addiction of opioid users and defrauded insurance companies out of millions of dollars. In effect, he was a major Atlantic County drug dealer.

And in the pill mill operation, the Pagans were his accomplices.

For the biker gang, it was simply a way to make money. And there was lots of money to be made. At the same time the Augello-Kauffman pill mill was operating in Atlantic County, members of the Philadelphia chapter of the Pagans got their hooks into another doctor who was more than willing to play along.

His name was William O'Brien III. Like Jim Kauffman, he was a doctor of osteopathic medicine. And like Jim Kauffman, he was attracted to the tough-guy image that was part of the biker underworld. O'Brien, overweight and nerdy, lacked the air of sophistication that Kauffman carried. But both doctors were drawn to the outlaw mystique that was part of the Pagans brand.

The case against O'Brien and nearly a dozen other Pagans and their associates was laid out in federal court in Philadelphia during a six-week trial that ended with O'Brien's conviction on more than 120 counts of drug dealing, conspiracy and contributing to the death of a patient. He was subsequently sentenced to thirty years in prison. All the other defendants in the case, including some key members of the biker gang, pled guilty before the case was put before a jury.

O'Brien opted to defend himself, a move that reinforced the old adage that a man who chooses to act as his own defense attorney has a fool for a client.

In this case, an arrogant fool.

"The depth and breadth of his criminality was astounding," US Attorney Zane Memeger said in a sentencing memorandum. "There was no explanation for his conduct other than unbridled, and amoral, greed."

At the time of his arrest in January 2015, O'Brien's bank account indicated he had just one hundred dollars on deposit. But during raids conducted at a home he shared with his girlfriend at the Jersey Shore and at a luxury condo in Philadelphia, authorities found expensive clothes and leather goods by designer labels like Prada, Chanel and Hermès, a $2,800 receipt for a purchase at Neiman Marcus and a $4,622.93 bill for repair work on a Mercedes-Benz. Evidence indicated O'Brien had taken two trips to Aruba and spent $15,000 on tickets to Philadelphia Eagles football games in 2014. Authorities said that when O'Brien was arrested, they found $10,290 hidden in furniture, another $3,000 in cash in his car and $1,256 on his person. What's more, authorities said his girlfriend had $114,950 in two bank safe-deposit boxes and $366,350 in five separate bank accounts.

His girlfriend pled guilty to money-laundering and bankruptcy-fraud charges.

The feds alleged that in 2014 alone, O'Brien wrote 4,663 prescriptions for controlled substances. His activity was so great that "Rite Aid Pharmacy decided they would no longer fill prescriptions" that he wrote, authorities noted. Prosecutors estimated that O'Brien wrote illegal scripts for 238,895 (30 milligram) oxycodone pills, 11,649 (15 mg) oxycodone tablets, 128,370 (10 mg) oxycodone pills and 160,492 (10 mg) methadone tablets in addition to prescriptions for Xanax, Percocet and other controlled substances. (At the time, authorities noted, the street sale value of a 30 mg oxycodone pill was twenty-five dollars. This would have put the street sales of the 30 mg pills alone at nearly $6 million.)

All of that activity, investigators said, was generated out of a "pill mill" O'Brien ran out of offices on Broad Street in South Philadelphia, on Bustleton Avenue in Northeast Philadelphia and in Trevose and Levittown, two suburbs of Philadelphia. According to the federal indictment, he was a major supplier in a conspiracy set up by members of the Pagans who operated out of a clubhouse near his Levittown office.

The scam was up and running between March 2012 and January 2015. During that period, the government contended, O'Brien knowingly wrote thousands of phony prescriptions for drugs that quickly ended up on the streets.

The economics of the scam was explained by a biker associate who later testified for the government at O'Brien's trial.

O'Brien charged $200 per visit but seldom bothered with a medical exam. The scripts were written for members of the Pagans or for "patients" who were working for the bikers. Those patients would be paid about $200 by their Pagan handler for having the scripts filled at local pharmacies and would then turn the pills over to the bikers.

"Forty patients at two hundred, that's eight thousand dollars a day," said a biker associate nicknamed Tomato Pie in detailing O'Brien's piece of the action. Tomato Pie, who testified for the government, also told the jury that O'Brien was fascinated with the biker underworld and "wanted power around him." He was constantly pestering Tomato Pie and others for biker paraphernalia, asking anyone and everyone to get him a Pagans T-shirt.

Although there is no indication O'Brien and Kauffman ever met, the two osteopaths shared a fascination with the biker underworld. They also saw the bikers as potential enforcers and problem solvers. Tomato Pie said O'Brien once asked him if he could arrange to have his first wife, from whom he had had a messy and costly divorce, killed . . . or at least badly beaten up.

"I told him he was crazy," Tomato Pie testified.

Jim Kauffman, of course, got a different answer from Freddy Augello.

Tomato Pie said the bikers tolerated O'Brien's sometimes outlandish behavior while ignoring his requests because "we had an investment in him." Like Kauffman in Atlantic County, O'Brien was a source of income for the bikers, a steady stream of cash built around the opioid crisis that was ripping the country apart.

In O'Brien's case, more so than in Kauffman's, the cash stream was often a river.

Over a two-year period outlined in the federal indictment, authorities said, Dr. William O'Brien III pocketed $1.8 million while his "patients," many of them members and associates of the Pagans, generated millions more in street sales. Some were pulling in as much as $10,000 a week, according to court documents.

In one of the seamier twists in the Philadelphia pill mill story, authorities said that while most of O'Brien's patients paid cash, the doctor developed a different payment plan for several go-go dancers who were sent to him by the Pagans. For those women, O'Brien would accept a blow job in exchange for a script.

Two testified at his trial.

One woman—a slim, dark-haired thirty-one-year-old who worked as a dancer in strip clubs—said she became addicted to the painkillers and became desperate when O'Brien told her he had run out of medical reasons to continue to prescribe the pills for her.

But he offered an alternative plan.

"He said that if I gave him a blow job he would continue to prescribe" oxycodone and methadone, she told the jury.

"I was so sick, I couldn't function without them," she said.

"I did things that I would never normally do," she said, acknowledging that she traded oral sex for scripts during several visits to the doctor's office. "I had no choice," she told the jury. "I couldn't get the medication" without a prescription. "I was in too deep."

When a prosecutor asked her if she wanted to perform oral sex on the doctor, the woman quietly replied, "No."

Another dancer told the jury that she sought O'Brien's help when she was six months pregnant and had the ugly track marks of her heroin addiction running down both her arms. She said she wanted methadone to help break her habit.

She said he told her he'd write a script . . . for a blow job.

She agreed.

"He locked the door," the woman said in recounting the incident for the jury. "He was standing with his back to the door. I was on my knees."

She remembered that he wasn't wearing a belt, which she thought was odd. She said he wanted to ejaculate in her mouth. She refused. She said he wanted to have sexual intercourse with her. She said not without a condom. He didn't have one.

She left with a script for 180 methadone tablets.

The sexual angle was further documented by an undercover woman FBI agent who was introduced into the scam by a cooperating witness. Each time the agent met with the doctor, she had a recording device in her handbag.

The evidence introduced during the trial included a taped conversation in which the woman agent asked for an increase in the Xanax O'Brien was prescribing. The larger dose was known as a "blue," apparently because of the color of the pill.

On the tape, which was played for the jury, O'Brien suggested "a blue for a blow." The agent turned down the offer.

But a federal prosecutor would tell the jury that several other women, some already addicted, did not or could not say no. Au-

thorities said there were several other strippers and go-go dancers who were also regular patients, most "referred" to O'Brien by
the Pagans. How many had had similar experiences could not be
determined, but the stories told under oath in open court and
detailed in government memos added a salacious twist to what
became known as a tale of "Pagans, Pills and Prostitutes."

In the Pagan underworld, women are property, so there was
little concern over any attempt by the doctor to take advantage
of the dancers and strippers who were part of the scam. Sex,
drugs and cash were commodities in a lucrative economic exchange.

There did come a time, however, when the scam nearly came
undone.

Money was the issue.

Sam Nocille was angry. Nocille, a leader of the Philadelphia
branch of the Pagans, was one of the bikers who set the O'Brien
pill mill operation in motion. But in 2013, he was sitting in
prison, doing time for a weapons offense. And, as sometimes
happens in the underworld, out of sight was out of mind.

His "brothers" in the club had stopped kicking up his share,
believed to be about $2,000 a week, from the pill mill scam.

Nocille, in phone calls from prison that were taped by authorities, went on a rant.

"All of a sudden he's changing the whole fuckin' thing," he
said in a call to his wife during which he complained about an
associate who was supposed to be minding the store while Nocille was away. "It's not gonna happen. . . . The door was opened
for him due to me."

In another call, Nocille told his wife, "I'm gonna split his fuckin' head open." He also indicated that he was less than pleased with the doctor, adding that "even that fat motherfucker Bill in Levittown is gonna get it.

"I ain't gonna be nice no more," Nocille said in another phone call. "I'm done with these fuckin' guys . . . making tons of money because of me. I opened the door for him real big."

The target of Nocille's ire, a Pagan associate, testified for the government in the O'Brien trial, admitting his role in the pill mill scam, implicating the doctor and the Pagans in the scheme and telling the jury that he left Philadelphia for a time because he feared for his life.

Nocille was never able to follow up on his threats, however. He died of a heart attack in prison in January 2014, shortly before he was to be released. He was forty-six.

The Nocille tapes were played at O'Brien's trial to help establish the relationship between the doctor and the bikers. O'Brien told the jury he had Pagans as patients but not as partners in any drug conspiracy. (A few years later, Kauffman would offer the same explanation.) The jury also heard a taped conversation from another Pagan, Patrick "Redneck" Treacy, in which he and his girlfriend discussed the oxycodone and Valium prescriptions he had obtained from "our friend in Levittown."

Treacy, an enforcer with the Pagans, was a regular patient of the doctor's. Prosecutors would describe him as one of the main collaborators in the pill mill operation. He and other members of the Pagans were referred to by Dr. O'Brien as "VIP patients" and often had access to the doctor's office through a private entrance, seldom having to sit in a waiting room, investigators said. Treacy's attitude and arrogance were highlighted in a government memo that focused on a "medical history" the bulky, tattooed Pagan had filled out during his first visit to O'Brien's office.

"Treacy mockingly reported on his intake form for the initial visit with O'Brien that he had been pregnant 'lots' of times, that he was menstruating and that recently he had had a 'PAP' test which screens for cervical cancer," prosecutors noted in the court document.

Notwithstanding those comments, authorities said, Treacy got a prescription for 240 oxycodone tablets and 60 Xanax during his first visit. Over the course of the investigation, authorities determined that Treacy had received scripts for at least 49,852 oxycodone pills and 17,070 methadone tablets. Treacy was sentenced to twenty years in prison following his own guilty plea in the case.

He also was a suspect, but never charged, in the murder of a patient who owed Dr. O'Brien $11,000, according to court documents. On a tape played at trial, O'Brien is heard threatening the patient, Anthony Rongione, telling him, "I'll hunt you down like a dog and hurt you."

Authorities said that Treacy and another Pagan, armed with a bat and a club, later confronted Rongione, but neighbors of the intended victim chased the bikers off. A few days later, however, Rongione and another man were found shot to death in Rongione's home. No one has ever been charged.

As he did with most of the allegations in the case, O'Brien sought to explain away his dispute with Rongione, telling the jury that the debt was merely $2,000 and that no one would ever be killed for that kind of money. Treacy, in a taped interview with the FBI, denied killing anyone.

Treacy's name also came up in the April Kauffman murder case. Andrew Glick said Treacy was one of the Pagans Freddy Augello contacted about the murder contract. Redneck turned down Augello's offer, Glick said.

"Nobody was gonna kill a woman for ten thousand dollars, which is what Freddy was offering," Glick said. "Some guys told Freddy they would do it for fifty thousand dollars or seventy-five thousand dollars, but Freddy wasn't gonna go for that because it would leave him with nothing. That's why he had to hire the junkie. He was the only one who would do it for ten thousand dollars."

Glick described Redneck as fearless. He said he was one of the toughest Pagans he had ever met and one of the few bikers he was actually afraid of. "He was somebody you didn't want to mess with," Glick said.

Redneck and the other Philadelphia Pagans tried to recruit Glick and some of his biker brothers in Cape May and Atlantic County into the Dr. O'Brien pill mill scheme.

"They wanted more people involved," Glick said. "It was a big moneymaker. But we passed. We had our own, smaller operation with Kauffman. Of course we didn't tell anybody that. We just said it was just too much of a hassle to ride into Philadelphia to get the scripts. Freddy never told the Mother Club about what we were doing because he didn't want to kick up any money. He was happy with what we had going."

The money wasn't nearly as much as what the Philadelphia bikers were sucking out of the O'Brien pill mill, but for Freddy Augello, who was always struggling for cash, it was more than enough.

"For the first time in his life, he was making significant money," Glick said.

In the Augello-Kauffman operation, testimony indicated, the doctor was writing bimonthly scripts for 120 pills for from ten to fifteen Augello associates. In the beginning of the scam, Kauffman was being paid a hundred dollars for each script he wrote, half of what O'Brien was charging in Philadelphia. But while O'Brien was pocketing tens of thousands of dollars a month, Kauffman at best was earning about $1,000 every other month. It was pocket change. Free money but nothing compared to the compound-cream scam, which some sources estimated was providing the doctor with more than $1,000 per patient per month. If Kauffman was writing scripts for just ten patients (and estimates were that he wrote for dozens), the compound-cream kickback would have been at least $10,000 a month. It was, sources believe, much more.

The other difference between the O'Brien and the Kauffman pill mills was the Pagans' take. In the Kauffman operation, it was considerably less. Those working with Augello in the scam would get the prescriptions filled. They then had two options, Glick said. They could give all the pills to Augello and, once he sold them, they would be paid $1,000. Or they could give Augello half the pills and keep the rest for themselves to sell or use.

Augello's take would range from $6,000 to $9,000 a month,

Glick said. At the low end, Freddy was pocketing more than $70,000 a year . . . tax free.

"It was more money than he had ever had," Glick said. "He was able to rent a house, something I don't think he had ever done before. Nice place. Three bedrooms. I think he was paying sixteen hundred dollars a month in rent. Without the pill mill, he could never have done that."

The Augello-Kauffman scheme started in 2011, around the same time that the Pagans in Philadelphia made their connections with O'Brien. Glick would describe it all from the witness stand several years later. He said Augello first heard about Kauffman from another biker, a kid named Stephen Wittenwiler Jr., who was an enforcer for Augello when Freddy headed the club. Wittenwiler had good bloodlines. His dad had been a Pagan nicknamed "Misfit." But it was the kid who really didn't fit in.

"He didn't ride a motorcycle," Glick said. "Freddy let him in the club because he was tough and would do whatever Freddy asked. He was about five foot ten and weighed nearly three hundred pounds. And he was ruthless. He was one of the guys Freddy would send to collect from the deadbeat gamblers that owed money to the mob. For a time, he was Freddy's sergeant at arms."

Stevie had a girlfriend, who was working as a temp at Kauffman's office, Glick said. Sometimes he would pick her up at work and would be wearing his Pagans T-shirt. Kauffman noticed and struck up a conversation. One thing led to another, Glick said, and soon Stevie was talking to Freddy about this doctor who was writing him scripts for oxycodone. Freddy saw the potential right away, but didn't want to share.

"There was this guy in the Herd, the support club, whose brother was a pharmaceutical rep," Glick said. "Freddy used him to get an introduction to the doc. Then he cut Stevie out of the deal. He started sending people in for scripts. I heard about it a few months later. By that point, Stevie was gone, not just from the pill mill, but from the club. Freddy decided that since Stevie didn't ride a bike, he couldn't be a Pagan. That was never an issue before, but now it mattered. That's the way Freddy operated. He was always for himself.

"If you were in a fight, Stevie was the guy you wanted with you. He would have been the best Pagan ever if he rode a motorcycle. If the Pagans were a car club, he would have been a lifetime member."

How and when Augello and Kauffman first met is still a matter of conjecture. Both men saw the value in keeping a low profile and staying in the shadows. Nor is it clear exactly when Kauffman first pitched a murder contract as part of the deal. But Glick said by 2012 it was known in the biker underworld that Freddy was looking for someone to kill the doctor's wife.

The money from the scripts and the promised $50,000 payment were part of the package. But there was even more. Playing off his vanity, Kauffman started to refer to Augello as "Hollywood," a nickname that pointed to Augello's self-image as a musician, artist and ladies' man. The nickname was clearly at odds with the "Miserable" moniker he carried in the biker under-world. Another part of the economic seduction that Kauffman used to pull Augello into the plot was what Glick described as a "goodwill gesture" at the beginning of the pill mill operation. Jim Kauffman, Glick said, gave Freddy a used Corvette, which Augello sold. Kauffman also promised to relocate Augello and set him up in business in Arizona. All Freddy had to do was have April Kauffman killed.

"This was Freddy's ticket out," Glick said. "That's why he always went along with the doc. A few days after the murder, when me and Slasher met with him, Freddy told us not to worry. If anybody asked all we had to say was we were the doc's pa-tients. He was treating us for diabetes, which in my case was true. He said as long as we stayed calm, nothing was gonna happen. Nobody would connect it to us.

"I didn't agree with that, but I wondered—and I still wonder—whether the doc had somebody high up who would make sure this case wouldn't get investigated. Was there somebody holding an umbrella over the doc, and did Freddy know about that, and was that why he wasn't worried? Didn't make sense to me that it took law enforcement so long to come after us.

"We never shut down the pill mill operation, and within a few months [of the murder], it was like nothing had happened. The money just kept rolling in. Different people got in and out of the deal. Freddy had a girlfriend and her daughter—they were both getting scripts."

The daughter, in her twenties, would later testify that she would bring half of the pills from her prescription to Augello. She said that she and Augello would meet on occasion at his sign-painting shop and that during those meetings she would give Augello a "massage" and he would give some of the pills back to her.

Like Dr. O'Brien, Augello was sometimes willing to negotiate drug deals for something other than cash.

EIGHT

I f James Kauffman was feeling any heat as the second anniversary of his wife's murder approached, it wasn't coming from law enforcement investigators. For reasons that were never clearly explained, the Atlantic County Prosecutor's Office appeared to be less than enthused about pursuing leads in the case. While information gathered in the first three months following the murder had laid out a road map toward what appeared to be a murder-for-hire case, no one seemed interested in putting the case together.

"This case was put on the shelf for a number of years," a detective involved in the investigation would later explain from the witness stand, adding that Atlantic County prosecutor James McClain "dictated everything that would happen on this case."

And in 2014 not a lot was happening.

McClain, who had been serving as acting Atlantic County

prosecutor for two years, was formally sworn in as the county's top law enforcement official in June of that year. A fifty-six-year-old career prosecutor, McClain had been in charge of the office since June 2012, serving in his acting capacity until his nomination by Governor Chris Christie was confirmed.

McClain, who declined to answer any questions about his role in the Kauffman murder case for this book, presided over what many perceived as a slow-moving investigation. That was what had prompted Pack's lawyers to complain that the information they were developing was falling on "deaf ears." Some within law enforcement circles had the same impression, raising questions about what they thought was a less-than-aggressive investigation.

Others, however, said McClain took a studied and professional approach, one that would be expected of a career law enforcement official. James Kauffman's own attorney, Edwin Jacobs Jr., was one of them.

"You don't get a medal for making imprudent charges," said Jacobs, who said that there were nearly a dozen search warrants aimed at James Kauffman during the investigation and that his client felt under intense pressure from law enforcement almost from the inception of the investigation. "I don't think [McClain] was dragging his feet at all."

Whether the pace of the investigation was based on prosecutorial caution that came with years of experience or whether other factors came into play remains an open question. McClain certainly had a solid track record. He began in the Atlantic County Prosecutor's Office in 1983, shortly after graduating from Rutgers Law School. He rose to the rank of the first assistant county prosecutor before being tapped by Christie to succeed Ted Housel, whose term expired in June 2012, just a month after April Kauffman was found dead. Prosecutors and judges in New Jersey are appointed rather than elected, to depoliticize the process. And while New Jersey's system does avoid the unseemly aspect of candidates for high law enforcement office soliciting political contributions and running election campaigns, the appointment process has its own political pitfalls. This would come into play much later in the Kauffman case.

McClain knew the way murder cases evolved. He had been the point man on one of the most notorious homicide investigations in Atlantic County history, concerning the 2010 abduction and murder of Martin Caballero, a grocery store owner from North Jersey who was carjacked in the garage of an Atlantic City casino-hotel while on his way to a birthday celebration there for his adult daughter.

Caballero was bludgeoned to death and his remains set afire. His burned-out car and charred remains were discovered on an Atlantic County farm road. Craig Arno, a drifter with family ties to the area, was charged with the crime. His girlfriend and accomplice, Jessica Kisby, was implicated in the case and later testified against Arno.

As a couple, Arno and Kisby were a low-life Bonnie and Clyde. To many they were an example of the dark side of the casino-gambling experiment. These were not the kind of people that legalized gaming was supposed to attract to the boardwalk to help rebuild the image and the economy of the struggling resort city. But like flies swarming around a piece of warm pie on a windowsill, grifters like Arno came with the gambling era.

Caballero was killed on a whim. His abductors had forced him to make a withdrawal from an ATM, a move that netted them $300. That was the maximum he could take. It was one of the most brutal and senseless murders of the Atlantic City casino era and one that attracted national attention. McClain cut a deal with Kisby in exchange for her testimony. She was eventually sentenced to thirty years in state prison. Arno got life.

McClain's no-nonsense handling of the case drew praise from both the media and law enforcement. He was perceived as a tough law-and-order prosecutor. All the more reason why his seeming reluctance to go full-bore in the April Kauffman murder investigation raised eyebrows.

In fact, the only place James Kauffman faced hard questions— and the only place he was publicly identified as a suspect in his wife's murder—was in the civil litigation in the life insurance dispute. The wrongful-death claim filed by Kim Pack's lawyer had laid out part of the case against the doctor. Pack's attorney would continue to gather information as the case moved forward. Depositions, formal question-and-answer sessions, would provide more details, but unlike the wrongful-death claim, which was a public record, the questions and answers given during the depositions would remain sealed. They were a prelude to an actual civil trial in which the question of who was entitled to the $600,000 in insurance payments would be resolved. The insurance company Transamerica had bowed out of the battle after winning court approval to place the money in an escrow account while the case wound its way through the courts.

In March of 2014 Kim Pack was formally deposed in the

case, answering questions for more than two hours from Jacobs. Four months later, in July, Jim Kauffman would be deposed by Pack's lawyer, Patrick D'Arcy. The questions and the answers during both sessions were pointed and at times disconcerting. But under the rules of civil litigation, none of it was made public.

In her deposition Kim Pack would repeat many of the things she had already told detectives. This allowed Kauffman to see in even greater detail what his stepdaughter was saying about him. Among other things, she expanded on the problems she had observed in her mother's troubled marriage. She offered a grim and depressing account of events that marred the relationship between James and April Kauffman, including an allegation that her mother had once discovered a used condom in James Kauffman's suitcase after he had returned from an out-of-town speaking engagement.

Kim Pack said her mother suspected Jim Kauffman slept with "hookers" while on his various business trips.

Pack was also questioned about another bump in the murder investigation that had occurred several months earlier when Detective Michael Mattioli, who had been on the case from its start, was reassigned. No official explanation has ever been offered, but Kim Pack was questioned about this during her deposition. She acknowledged that on occasion, during Mattioli's interaction with her, the detective had consoled her, hugged her and kissed her. But under questioning from Edwin Jacobs, she denied their relationship went any further and said she was not aware that he had been taken off the investigation because of a possible personal relationship with her.

"You had no species of sexual contact with him?" Jacobs asked.

"No," Pack replied.

"Okay," said Jacobs. "And nothing that you did was intended to influence the investigation?"

"No, sir," said Pack.

A few minutes later in the deposition, Jacobs returned to the sexual question, asking directly if Pack had engaged in sex, "oral, vaginal or otherwise," with Mattioli.

"No, sir," Pack replied. "No, sir."

When Jacobs asked if their relationship was the reason Mattioli had been removed from the case, Pack said, "You would have to ask Jim McClain that question. I don't know."

Jacobs said, "Well, I have." But he left it at that and did not offer any other details. "Didn't Investigator Mattioli tell you his misconduct with you is the exact reason he was taken off the case?" Jacobs then asked.

"No," Pack replied. "I haven't had discussions with him as to why he was taken off the case. After he was taken off the case, I had no further contact with him."

In an interview five years after the deposition, Jacobs declined to elaborate on what he knew about Mattioli's removal, but said that "Jim McClain would not have removed the chief investigator from the case without having a good reason for doing that."

Mattioli did not respond to a request for an interview for this book.

Jacobs also said the "touchy-feely, kissy-facey relationship" between Pack and Mattioli would have, in his estimation, raised questions about any information Mattioli turned up during the probe. It would have been "germane to his believability" and to his credibility, Jacobs added.

Jacobs's line of questioning at the deposition underscored the salacious, soap-opera-like backstory that had always been part of the April Kauffman murder investigation. The victim's "swinging lifestyle," her multiple sex partners, her seemingly open marriage were part of a rumor-and-innuendo mill that began churning on the day April Kauffman was found dead on the floor of her bedroom. Some believed the loose and at times outlandish talk was intended to discredit or besmirch the murder victim, to show that what had happened to her was brought about by her own actions, that somehow she had contributed to her own murder.

Now her daughter was facing a line of questioning that indirectly reinforced that perception. Everyone knew there was bad blood between Kim Pack and Jim Kauffman. Her claims in the civil suit, he would argue through his lawyer, were just part of a money grab, a way for her to get the $600,000 in insurance. She was saying and doing whatever she could to discredit him and to blame him for her mother's murder. The implication in the questions about Mattioli went even further. Now Kauffman, through his lawyer, was hinting that his stepdaughter had been using sex to influence the murder investigation.

When Kauffman was deposed in July, the story he told in response to questions asked by Patrick D'Arcy included several details that were at odds with his initial statements to the police. Among other things, by 2014 Kauffman was saying that he had, in fact, rushed to his wife's side when he saw her lying on the floor of their bedroom and had immediately checked her pulse. That, he said, was when he realized she was dead. On the day of the murder, he had told Detective Mattioli that he hadn't touched the body, but he had known from his experience as a doctor that his wife was dead.

The deposition on July 11 covered much of the same ground that Mattioli had explored in the early days of the investigation. But in this version, Kauffman said he and April had slept in the same bed that night. He didn't recall what they had had for dinner. No mention of cooking steaks on the grill. But he again said they had made love before going to sleep. No mention of any time in the Jacuzzi, however.

He said when he had gotten to the home on the morning of the murder, he rushed upstairs to his wife's side. He felt her neck for a pulse and realized that she was dead.

"She had the pallor and no pulse, and she was cold," Kauffman said in describing what he saw and felt that morning. Then, he said, "I ran downstairs and went out on the lawn and was hysterical and started vomiting."

Millie Tate had come up to him at that point, but he didn't remember what he had said to her. He also said he had not sat in his Ford Explorer talking on the cell phone, nor had he looked down the street before rushing into the house, which is what Tate had told Mattioli she witnessed that morning.

He also said April took "prodigious amounts of Valium" to help her sleep. He admitted calling in a prescription in her name for medication he took, but said that was "an accident," that he was so used to calling in scripts for others that he mistakenly used his wife's name instead of his own when he ordered a ten-day supply of antidepressants. He said April had not been pressuring him for a divorce. On the contrary, he said they were talking about downsizing and setting up a lifestyle that would allow them to spend more time in Arizona. And while he admitted that he had no military background, he implied that he let others believe that because it helped in the work he and April were doing for veterans. In fact, he said, it was he who set April on that path.

"I was big into quietly doing things for the veterans," he said. "And at that time, it [claiming to have been in the military] helped me get the veterans to get some better care, and then April picked up the ball and ran with it. And we did very well helping the veterans."

While others might have thought he served in the military, he said April knew he had not. He said he had told her within the first year of her marriage. This, of course, conflicted with reports that April was both embarrassed and distraught when she learned shortly before she was killed that her husband's claims of military service were bogus.

Asked if he had ever threatened to "go nuclear" on April and her family if she pushed for a divorce, Kauffman replied, "Well, I've never used the term 'nuclear,' so the answer is no."

"Did you ever threaten to shoot April?" D'Arcy asked as a prelude to questions about the Egg Harbor Township police report that focused on the 2006 incident.

"Absolutely not," Kauffman replied.

He admitted he had had an angry phone conversation with his friend after learning that his friend's twenty-two-year-old son had been discovered "making out" with April. He said that his son-in-law had told him in a phone call and that he, in turn, had called his friend. But he said he had never threatened to put a bullet in April's head or to shoot his friend's son, as the police report indicated.

"So he's mistaken when he went to the police department and wrote out a sworn statement and said that you threatened to put a bullet in April's head?" D'Arcy asked.

"That's correct. . . . I categorically deny ever saying I would kill my wife," Kauffman replied.

"Okay," said D'Arcy. "And obviously, then, it goes without saying that you never threatened to kill April Kauffman to her face, correct?"

"Never," said the doctor.

"You never threatened to kill Kim Pack to April, correct?" asked the lawyer.

"Never," said the doctor.

The deposition lasted about four hours and included several other insights into the doctor's life and character. He said he had not spoken to his elderly mother, Ruth, for about a year, explaining that "over the last fifty or sixty years my mother has said some inappropriate things, and it finally got to a head, and I said I really don't think I want to continue this discussion right now."

He also said he was estranged from his two daughters from his first marriage, which had ended in divorce nearly twenty years earlier. He hadn't spoken to his children in "eight to ten years," he said, adding that they had "defected to their mother."

Asked if he would describe his marriage to April as "happy"

prior to the murder, Kauffman said, "As happy as every other marriage . . . Everybody has ups and downs."

Throughout what amounted to a daylong session, Kauffman repeatedly denied that he had had anything to do with his wife's murder. Finally, D'Arcy asked him who he thought might have killed April.

He said that he had gone over that with his lawyer and that he believed Jacobs had forwarded that information to the Atlantic County Prosecutor's Office. Jacobs, who was present during the questioning, objected and said lawyer-client confidentiality prohibited Kauffman from disclosing what he had told his lawyer.

"I debriefed my client in an effort to assist the prosecutor," Jacobs said. "And after debriefing my client, I passed information to the prosecutor." This would have been in the form of a letter that Jacobs sent to the prosecutor's office on October 4, 2012. The contents of that letter have never been publicly disclosed.

But at the deposition, D'Arcy was able to get around the lawyer-client issue when Kauffman acknowledged that he had discussed possible murder suspects with Carole Weintraub while they were dating and before they were married. He said he raised the possibility of a troubled veteran with whom April might have come in contact or someone she had clashed with through her radio broadcasts, maybe someone who was "anti-veteran," he said. He also raised the possibility of police involvement, claiming April had been the target of harassment by the Linwood police for several years because of her outspoken criticism of the department. Finally, he said, there might have been someone with a motorcycle gang.

"What motorcycle gang?" D'Arcy asked.

"The Pagans," said the doctor.

"Why would you think that?"

"She had some bizarre relationship with somebody in the Pagans who I've met a couple of times," said Kauffman. "And it just didn't seem appropriate. . . . I met him twice. . . . It has to be a year or so before her passing. We were in Smithville. She said there was a meeting with the Pagans and there was some music or something, so I went along with her. And there was a whole group of Pagans sitting there, which is not my social circle of motorcycle riders."

This would seem to be an oblique reference to Fred Augello, a Pagan and a musician. Kauffman did not offer any additional details about the individual, but a cousin of Augello's said that Augello's mother and April's grandmother—the woman who had raised her—were lifelong friends. That was one potential link between Augello and April Kauffman. Another was that both had graduated from Holy Spirit High School, although they were there at different times. Augello was about ten years older than April.

In his deposition, James Kauffman said he owned two motorcycles.

"I had one, and she had one," he said of April.

"The Pagans is a motorcycle gang?" Kauffman was asked.

"According to what I see on TV and in the papers, they are more than just a motorcycle gang."

"Right," said D'Arcy. "You don't have any contact with them?"

"None whatsoever," Kauffman replied.

"You don't have any patients that are Pagans, or anything like that?"

"If I do, I don't know they are. . . . They don't show up with their colors on."

Andrew Glick and Fred Augello would later agree that the doctor was attempting to throw them under the bus and divert attention from his own involvement in the murder of his wife. But in the summer of 2014, when Dr. James Kauffman gave his deposition, authorities were still a long way from putting a case together.

As a result, the murder of April Kauffman had virtually no impact on the pill operation that was putting money in the pockets of Augello and Glick. The economic arrangements, however, had changed. About a year after the murder, around the same time he went to war with the insurance company over his dead wife's death benefit payments, Jim Kauffman decided he wanted out of the drug ring.

Glick was making a regular visit to the doctor's office, where he was receiving treatment for his diabetes and also receiving his bimonthly script for 120 oxycodone tablets.

"I feel I have met my responsibility," Glick said the doctor told him while announcing that he was no longer going to write the opioid prescriptions. This reinforced Glick's belief that the only reason Kauffman had set up the pill mill was to get someone to kill his wife. But Glick wasn't about to let the doctor walk. He said as much. Kauffman then countered with a proposal that he hoped might force the bikers to bow out of the deal.

"He said that instead of one hundred dollars for each script he wrote, he wanted five hundred dollars," Glick said. "I thought it was bullshit, but when I talked to Freddy, he said we should go along with it. I said I'd rather strangle him, but Freddy didn't want to lose the income, so we started paying him five hundred dollars for each script."

By that point, the number of patients involved in the scam had dropped from fifteen to eight. Kauffman, who was making $800, was now going to receive $4,000. The money would come out of the pockets of Augello and Glick. Glick's take from the pill mill operation would drop to about $900 a month. Freddy's would go down to about $3,200. For Glick, who said he was making about $18,000 a month selling meth and coke, it wasn't about the money. It was the principle.

Glick didn't feel the doctor should have been able to dictate terms. He and Augello were the outlaws. They were the ones who should have been establishing the rules, not an endocrinologist with a biker fantasy who didn't have the guts to kill his wife himself, but was happy to have the Pagans do it for him.

"The doc was just an arrogant guy," Glick said. "I think he thought Freddy wouldn't agree to the five hundred and that would be the end of it. To tell you the truth, I didn't really care about the money. I just didn't like him telling us what to do."

For Glick, vice was commerce. It was as simple as that. He never really thought about the moral or social implications of dealing drugs. If he wasn't supplying, someone else would. That was the way he looked at it.

And when it came to opioids, he didn't see the harm. Early in the scam, he had made a connection with a guy who had been getting oxycodone from a source in Florida. Glick offered to sell him his pills—120 every other month—and the guy eagerly went along.

"He had two rich women from Avalon [a posh South Jersey shore community] who were buying from him," Glick said. "They paid cash, and it was never a problem. These were the kind of women who never had to worry about money. I guess they didn't want their husbands to know they were using. If I wasn't supplying the drugs, they'd get them somewhere else. To me, it was just income."

Jim Kauffman continued to write scripts for the pill mill operation for the next four years, but during that time he found even more lucrative sources of illegal income. Court documents that would surface in both the Kauffman murder case and two medical insurance–fraud investigations linked James Kauffman to two moneymaking schemes that had nothing to do with dirty scripts or the Pagans.

Much of the information was contained in a search warrant affidavit, a sworn statement of probable cause, written by Detective James N. Scoppa Jr., who took over as lead investigator in the Kauffman murder case after Mattioli was removed from the investigation.

Scoppa had worked in the Atlantic County Prosecutor's Gangs, Guns and Narcotics Unit before moving over to Major Crimes. His thirty-page affidavit offered a detailed look at the allegations swirling around James Kauffman, starting with the murder of his wife and including allegations that the doctor was operating a pill mill with the Pagans and taking kickbacks in two more elaborate medical insurance–fraud schemes, one involving writing scripts for unnecessary blood tests and the other involving bogus scripts for compound pain creams. Both schemes, authorities would allege, generated tens of thousands of dollars in payoffs and would help explain reports that on any given day the doctor would have from $10,000 to $80,000 in cash in his office or in his home.

In writing about the warrant, the *Press of Atlantic City*, the local newspaper that provided extensive coverage of the April Kauffman murder investigation, described Kauffman as a "one-man crime spree."

The blood tests were paid for in many cases by Medicare and Medicaid and for a time were conducted by a lab company that Kauffman was permitted to set up within his own medical office complex. More lucrative still was his apparent involvement in a multimillion-dollar insurance-fraud scam involving compound pain creams and lotions. Insurance companies were bilked out of nearly $50 million for the prescriptions written to treat bogus ailments of patients who sometimes were never even examined.

Both the blood-testing scheme and the compound-cream scam were being investigated by federal authorities who clearly provided information that Scoppa included in his affidavit.

"Based upon a lengthy FBI investigation, Dr. James Kauffman has been identified as a suspect in an additional pharmaceutical/healthcare [sic] fraud involving compounding medications," Scoppa wrote.

"The fraud entails compounded medications being written to patients, with kickbacks to the physicians in a manner similar [to the blood lab] kickback fraud," the affidavit read in part. "As such, patients are receiving unnecessary treatments, medication or tests, in exchange for pecuniary gain. The pharmaceutical company, through a recruiter or intermediary, in turn pays the doctor who wrote the prescriptions. Ultimately, recruiters of patients, or 'straw patients,' and/or patients receive a cash payment in relation to the number of prescriptions they have ordered."

The search warrant alleged that Kauffman wrote more than seven hundred scripts for unneeded lotions and creams in a scheme that included a rogue pharmaceutical company that manufactured tubes of medication that sometimes cost as little as ten dollars. The company would bill unsuspecting insurance companies as much as $10,000 per tube. Scripts in the scheme were often written for a year's supply (twelve tubes) of the medication. Those involved included pharmaceutical representatives who helped put the scam in motion, doctors who wrote the scripts and "patients" who made the insurance claims. Everyone received a piece of the action.

How much Kauffman made through the blood-test and compound-cream scams has never been made public. Kauffman died before he could be charged. But one intriguing piece of potential evidence turned up when investigators found records of a series of text messages sent on October 6, 2015, from a lab owner/operator who eventually pleaded guilty to fraud in the blood-test scam. The texts implied that Kauffman had ended his business deal with the operator who had set up a lab in Kauffman's office and that Kauffman had gone with one of the operator's rivals.

The message warned that Kauffman's new partner was working with the feds and might be wearing a body wire. "Good luck, you'll be in prison real soon," the message read in part.

The lab owner also berated Kauffman for turning his back on

him, implying that Kauffman had a reputation for only caring about himself. "Now I understand why all the other doctors . . . don't talk to you anymore. And you know what, I don't blame them."

The lab owner was not the only individual linked to the scams who pleaded guilty. Several individuals involved in the compound-cream scam took pleas. One pharmaceutical rep at the top of the criminal chain, Matthew Tedesco, pleaded guilty to conspiracy to commit insurance fraud. His take from the scheme, according to his plea agreement in federal court, was $11,166,844.20. Three other individuals, two of whom admitted to "recruiting patients," were charged with illegal earnings of $388,608, $179,370 and $89,855. How much Kauffman made from the scheme has yet to be made public, although Glick said he believes it was more than a million dollars.

Various versions of the same scheme have played out across the country. One infamous case involved the bilking of millions from an insurance carrier for military personnel. Another, in Tampa, focused on $157 million in insurance payments for bogus claims in a scheme that federal authorities said had organized-crime connections. An insurance watchdog group has called compound cream "the snake oil of the twenty-first century."

"In general, compounding was a practice in which a licensed pharmacist combines, mixes, or alters ingredients of one or more drugs in response to a prescription to create a medication tailored to the medical needs of an individual patient," federal prosecutors wrote in the document charging Tedesco with insurance fraud.

While the drug combination might not be FDA approved, the

prosecutors noted, it could be "appropriately prescribed by a physician when an FDA-approved medication did not meet the health needs of a particular patient. For example, if a patient was allergic to a specific ingredient in an FDA-approved medication, such as a dye or preservative, a compounded drug could be prepared excluding the ingredient that triggers the allergic reaction."

That was the loophole on which the various scams—which nationally have totaled hundreds of millions in insurance fraud—were based.

The Atlantic County scam in which Kauffman was involved focused on public employees—policemen, firemen, schoolteachers—whose taxpayer-financed insurance policies covered compound-cream prescriptions.

Those government workers "were recruited" by individuals working with Tedesco, authorities alleged, and received kickbacks for their involvement. Many got their prescriptions from Jim Kauffman. In almost every case, authorities said, the patient "had no medical necessity for the compound medication."

Andrew Glick laughed and shook his head when comparing the pill mill to the compound-cream scam.

"The pain cream was big money," he said almost wistfully while acknowledging that the insurance he carried from his job as a chef would never have approved such payments.

"If I had asked for something like that, my insurance company would have told me to go buy a tube of Bengay," he said.

NINE

Kim Pack and her attorney continued to beat the drum about the seemingly stalled murder investigation, using both social media and the press to keep the story front and center. At the same time, pressure was building in the medical insurance–fraud probe that focused on the compound-cream and blood-testing scams. And while those were federal cases, savvy Atlantic County investigators saw them as a way to get into the murder investigation through a back door.

If, as it appeared, there was reluctance on the part of the Atlantic County Prosecutor's Office to aggressively pursue the April Kauffman homicide and if, as many investigators had come to believe, James Kauffman was the primary suspect, then putting pressure on Kauffman for any reason could pay dividends.

Another rich area of information, if not hard, cold evidence, was the civil litigation over the $600,000 in life insurance. Jim Kauffman's grab for that money had opened another door for authorities who were tracking the case. And in March of 2015, Carole Weintraub was reluctantly dragged through it.

She was deposed on March 12, questioned for nearly three hours by Patrick D'Arcy, Pack's lawyer. Her answers offered nothing new about the murder itself. Carole was as much in the dark as everyone else. But they did provide more insight into the life and times, the quirks and habits, of James Kauffman. And as any good investigator knows, understanding your target and what motivates him is half the battle.

Carole's videotaped deposition, similar to the ones Kim Pack and James Kauffman had been subject to several months earlier, focused on Jim Kauffman's "military service," an issue that Pack and authorities believed was a motive for the murder. While Kauffman had said April knew the claim was bogus and went along with it, investigators saw it as one of the reasons Kauffman wanted his wife dead. Her discovery of her husband's stolen-valor claim late in their marriage was added ammunition she had hoped to use to force him to divorce her. It was a betrayal of everything she had worked for, and it was personally embarrassing.

Carole Weintraub was perplexed and surprised by the information D'Arcy offered through the questions he posed. But at this point, she was still adamant in defending her husband. She acknowledged that she had read something in the newspaper about him serving as a Green Beret, but never believed it. And in response to one of the first questions she was asked, she said her husband had never told her he was in the military.

D'Arcy quoted from the college paper Kim Pack had written in which Jim Kauffman talked at length about his military exploits, about how "he was a Vietnam vet and that his battalion had been wiped out and he played dead because the Vietcong was [sic] nearby. But he was able to obtain the dog tags of all of his fellow soldiers, and he was able to escape into the jungle, where he remained for several days but was then rescued."

Carole said she had never heard that story and did not believe he had ever served in the military.

"Okay. So this is, this is news to you, that he had told other people that he was a Green Beret, right?" D'Arcy asked.

Carole started laughing.

"Yes," she said.

"Is that funny?" D'Arcy asked.

"Yes," she said. When asked why, she explained, "I just don't think he's that sort of person . . . that he would volunteer to be a Green Beret or even volunteer for the military."

When D'Arcy asked what kind of person she thought would volunteer, she quickly replied, "Somebody who doesn't mind getting shot at."

At another point, the lawyer also asked if she knew James Kauffman had been forced to withdraw from college because of poor grades. Carole said she knew his grades had been bad but said that she believed his withdrawal was also due to a lack of money.

The lawyer then showed her a college transcript that indicated that on May 31, 1969, the committee on academic standards ruled that James Kauffman "was required to withdraw for academic reasons." He was later readmitted, but finished his career at Franklin & Marshall with a cumulative grade point average of 2.09, which ranked him "432 to 441 out of 459 kids," D'Arcy said.

In response to another question, Carole said she did not know that her husband had undergone a military exam as part of the draft process in the late 1960s and had been declared 4-F, unfit for service.

Nor was she aware that while applying to medical school, Kauffman had written a letter to the Philadelphia College of Osteopathic Medicine in which he apparently tried to explain away his poor college grades.

"I decided to go to a psychiatrist," he wrote. "That decision was one of the hardest I have ever made. It was also the turning point of my life. I went almost a year trying to put back the pieces of a shattered life. I learned I was not psychotic but had an emotional maladjustment due to my environment at home. But most importantly, I learned how to face this problem and any other that might arise."

What D'Arcy was establishing was obvious. James Kauffman made up stories in order to cast himself in the best light and hid the truth when it made him look bad. He had done it with April and, it would seem, he had also done it with Carole.

Carole said she never knew he had been treated by a psychiatrist but was not surprised by the assessment. Jimmy, she said, "grew up in a very difficult and sad household."

D'Arcy asked what was sad about it, and Carole told him that her husband's father "was the only survivor on a boat on D-Day" that had had twenty-eight men aboard. So he always suffered from guilt.

The lawyer also asked for details about the rekindled relationship, coming back repeatedly to the fact that the romance had begun just weeks after the murder. "Did you ever have an affair with Jim Kauffman while he was married?" the lawyer asked.

"No," she said.

Then he asked about her engagement ring.

"Did you ever know that he traded in some of the jewelry of his [late] wife and then got jewelry back and gave it to you?" the lawyer said. "Did he [Kauffman] ever tell you that?"

He had not, she said.

Had her husband ever threatened her physically?

"Never," she said.

Had she ever considered the possibility that James Kauffman had something to do with his wife April's murder?

"Never," she said.

Had she ever asked her husband about the murder?

She said she had not wanted to upset her husband, who she believed was still dealing with the trauma, and so she never probed.

"To put it bluntly," D'Arcy then inquired, did that mean that she was "not really interested?"

Carole bristled at the question and the suggestion it carried.

"I'd like to correct your characterization," she said. "I am interested in how it affected my husband and the toll it took on him."

Asked to describe that toll, she said, "Well, for a man whose wife was murdered, I think he's done pretty well under the circumstances. He's maintained his work. He's never missed a day of work, except when he was—once or twice when he was sick. . . . He maintained his relationships, and he just put one foot in front of the other and just got through the day."

The deposition lasted nearly three hours and included questions about Kauffman once threatening to put a bullet in April's head after the affair in 2006 with the twenty-two-year-old. Carole said she knew nothing about that incident or of any threats.

In another question that would figure prominently in the murder investigation, D'Arcy asked her about a cell phone—a throwaway phone, he called it; a "burner phone" in police jargon. D'Arcy said there had been more than three hundred calls between that phone and James Kauffman between August 18, 2011, and May 9, 2012, the day before the murder. Carole did not recognize the number and had no idea who owned the cell phone.

D'Arcy had clearly been doing his homework . . . or had been given some information by investigators. (The actual number of calls, according to testimony at Augello's trial, was 276.) While it was not public information at the time, that cell phone, authorities would later allege, was controlled by Freddy Augello. And while Augello and James Kauffman seldom met face-to-face, investigators believed they communicated on that cell phone line. Calls were tracked coming from the phone to Kauffman and from Kauffman to the phone. It was one of the few hard pieces of evidence tying the doctor to the biker. None of that was hinted at during the deposition, but the question clearly foreshadowed where authorities were heading.

D'Arcy continued to poke at Carole's relationship with her husband and came back again and again to the timing of the romance in the wake of the murder. She told him she thought

April Kauffman
Media Pool Augello Trial

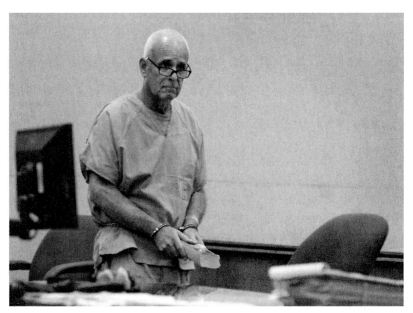
Dr. James Kauffman enters the courtroom.
Media Pool Pretrial Hearing

Joseph "Irish" Mulholland testified that he served as a reluctant getaway driver for the murderer.

Media Pool Augello Trial

Carole Weintraub's high school portrait.
She knew James Kauffman at that time,
but she felt reconnecting with him later
was a mistake.

Courtesy of Carole Weintraub Kauffman

Fred Augello at the defense table. He ran the pill mill and was convicted of organizing April Kauffman's murder.

Media Pool Augello Trial

Andrew Glick testifies. A friend of Freddy Augello's, he agreed to cooperate with the government and testify against him.
Media Pool Augello Trial

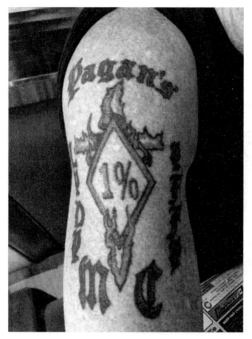

Andrew Glick's Pagan's tattoo. On the left side it reads *LPDP* (Live a Pagan, Die a Pagan). On the right, *PFFP* (Pagan Forever, Forever Pagan).

George Anastasia

April Kauffman's daughter, Kim Pack, makes a victim statement in the courtroom.

Media Pool Augello Trial

he was "being trite" when he appeared to be going overboard about dates, timing and Jewish customs, but she continued to answer his questions.

At one point Carole said her husband had theorized about who might have been behind the murder, echoing some of what he had said during his own deposition—a disgruntled veteran, the police or someone from April's social set.

She said one of her husband's lawyers had made reference to the Pagans, but she had never heard that specifically from her husband. She also said the lawyer Louis Barbone had told her that April and the Linwood chief of police had had an ongoing "feud" and that April had once been wrongly arrested. This may have been related to a dispute April had had after divorcing her second husband, also a doctor, and to a restraining order he had obtained. But the deposition questions went no further on that topic.

Carole was reluctant to talk about her husband's murdered wife. When pressed by D'Arcy, she fell on the legalese that lawyers often use. Anything she had ever heard about April Kauffman was "just hearsay." She knew nothing firsthand.

Did her husband ever tell her he was going to divorce April? she was asked.

"No, I never heard that," she said.

Before he finished, D'Arcy again came back to the stolen-valor issue, saying, "Well, you're an intelligent woman. Give me a good reason that someone would tell people they were a war hero."

Carole tried to defend her husband in the face of facts that made a defense difficult.

"I don't know," she said. "But I will say this, Mr. D'Arcy. What he did in his past was the past. And we just decided to move forward from the time that we reunited."

But D'Arcy wasn't willing to let it go at that and tried to get her to admit that what people have done in their past could matter.

Carole was forced to agree.

"Yeah, I mean, if he robbed a train," she said.

"Or killed someone?" the lawyer added.

"He didn't," Carole said.

Carole had defended her husband throughout the deposition but came away from the experience somewhat unnerved. She decided it was time to confront her husband on some of those issues. The first thing she asked him about was the canard about his military service and the stories about him being a war hero.

"I told Jimmy I read about him being a Green Beret in a local rag and laughed when I saw it," she said. She reminded him that the boy she dated was more concerned about dodging the draft than enlisting.

"It was ludicrous to think he was a Green Beret," she said, pointing out that the documents uncovered by D'Arcy clearly indicated he was "anxiously awaiting a letter from selective service, hoping he wouldn't get drafted."

But she was shocked to find out, as D'Arcy had explained to her during the deposition, that her husband had bought himself some military gear to continue his pose as a war hero, including fake medals and a green beret.

"I just looked at him and said, 'How could you do something like that?'

"'I just did it,'" she said he replied.

"That was really wrong," she told him, especially to the "people who sacrificed so much."

He promptly offered up a cover story that spread the blame for his stolen-valor crimes to his late wife, the same story he had told during his own deposition. It was a "joint decision" between him and April and was designed to lend credibility to his wife's campaign to help veterans.

"'It just got out of hand,'" Carole said he told her.

Even though it had not come up in her deposition, she also asked about the rumors surrounding the pill mill and the Pagans, allegations that had not resulted in any charges, but that had been hinted at as the murder investigation stalled.

"Here's this man committed to healing people and making them better," Carole said. "And on the flip side, he's writing prescriptions that would have hurt or even killed somebody? Had I known that, it would have been the end of our relationship."

But James Kauffman, the smartest guy in the room, was always in charge, with his patients and with his wife. He had an explanation for everything. It was true, he said, that some of his patients were Pagans. But they didn't have health insurance. He was just doing them a favor and was treating them for their medical problems.

Carole accepted the explanation, telling herself, "Pagans get sick too."

But the deposition and her husband's subsequent explanations had planted doubt. Carole began to wonder if the Jimmy Kauffman she had married was the Jimmy Kauffman she had known forty years earlier.

Andrew Glick, on the other hand, had no doubts about who James Kauffman was. The "doc" was a central figure in the pill mill operation and the man behind the murder of his wife. But from where Glick was standing, it didn't seem either of those crimes would ever lead to an arrest.

Everything else was just noise, and he was happy to be above the fray.

He was not concerned about the federal investigations into the medical insurance fraud. That was something for Jim Kauffman to worry about. And he had no dog in the life insurance fight that pitted Kauffman against Kim Pack.

So for a time, at least, Glick was able to relax. He and his wife, Vicky, had moved into a new $300,000 home on seven acres just off Ridge Avenue in Egg Harbor Township. The sprawling ranch-style home with the swimming pool in the backyard was just a few miles down the road from Storybook Land, a popular children's amusement park built around fairy-tale characters.

Glick would smile and shake his head when he drove past the entrance to the park. Those characters and the outlandish stories around which they were built weren't that far removed from the people and events he was dealing with regularly in the biker underworld.

Glenn "Slasher" Seeler and his wife, Cheryl Pizza, who had been part of the pill mill operation, had left town. Glick liked Slasher but wasn't sorry to see him go. He thought Cheryl was trouble, but there wasn't much he could do about it. Love—or lust—sometimes clouds the mind.

"They were living in this boardinghouse in Ocean City," Glick said. "They used to invite me over. They lived in one room. Bathroom down the hall. They wanted me to hang out with them. You had to sit on the bed. It was like living in a college dorm."

In November of 2013 police raided the boardinghouse and arrested Seeler and Pizza. A newspaper report said the arrests capped an ongoing drug investigation.

Police seized four handguns, a stun gun "and drug paraphernalia commonly used for the distribution, packaging and sale of controlled substances." Seeler was described in the report as a "known gang member."

"Someone had made an undercover buy from Glenn," Glick said. "He was selling cocaine that he got from me, not a lot but enough to make some money. When they arrested him, they tried to get him to talk about the Kauffman case, but he didn't give anything up. He knew the drug case against him wasn't a big deal. In fact, he and Cheryl both got probationary sentences, no jail time. They walked away."

Seeler was no dummy. He knew he was a person of interest in the murder investigation and figured it might be smart to get out of town. He and his wife relocated to North Carolina. But things didn't get any better there. Slasher could be somewhat domineering, and the couple got into a domestic dispute over some phone records. Slasher suspected Cheryl was running around, and when he checked her cell phone, he saw messages that he said confirmed his suspicions.

Both would later offer accounts of what happened next. Depending on which version was being offered, Cheryl either was locked in a bedroom by her husband or locked herself in to get away from her husband.

A gunshot quickly followed.

"I accidentally shot Glenn through a closed door," Cheryl Pizza said.

Pizza said she was frightened after being locked in the bedroom. She said she didn't have a key, so she took the handgun they kept in the room and tried to shoot off the lock on the door. She said she had warned Glenn that she was going to shoot the doorknob. "I told him about ten times" before pulling the trigger, she said.

Slasher said that there was no warning, that the shot came out of nowhere. He said he was standing outside the bedroom door when a bullet ripped into his abdomen.

"She shot me over it," he said of the cell phone message dispute. "I'm missing four feet of my intestines. Not fun." He survived the shooting, but the marriage didn't. A few years later he was still using a cane to get around.

Fairy tales?

Happy endings?

Pizza was arrested, and said she spent three months in a county jail. She was later sentenced to time served and placed on probation. The couple split up after that. Slasher stayed in North Carolina, while Pizza moved to South Carolina. That was where they were living when they were scooped up in the Kauffman murder case a few years later.

Seeler's decision to leave the Atlantic City area eliminated one of the conduits that Fred Augello was using to communicate with Jim Kauffman. Slasher said he used to take messages to the doctor from Augello. He did this on nearly a dozen occasions, he said, never bothering to read the notes before handing them to Kauffman.

"He would open it up, read it and put it in his pocket," Slasher later testified. Asked if he ever opened up any of the notes and read them, Slasher replied, "I'm not a curious person."

Glenn "Slasher" Seeler was a biker in every sense of the word, Glick said. He understood the underworld and was a willing player in it. Glick said he couldn't say that for some of the others he had had to deal with. But it all came with the territory. Glick was the president of the chapter and was expected to deal with all the issues, major and minor, that came with wearing the diamond.

He had succeeded Augello as president, and he had inherited Kauffman and the pill mill along with everything else that came with being in charge.

"Hope for the best and plan for the worst," he said. "That's the way I looked at things."

Years later he still spoke with pride about his life in the biker underworld, the "brotherhood" he found in being a Pagan and the loyalty and respect that came with his role as the president of a chapter.

He had been formally initiated into the Pagans during a biker run to Charleston, West Virginia, in April 2008. The "ceremony" took place in a motel bar just outside of Charleston, he said with a smile. Guys were drinking shots all night and periodically one of the prospects who had been proposed for membership would be called up to the bar, where one of the leaders of the Mother Club was holding court.

Glick's turn came a little before midnight. He was summoned by a burly biker boss who appeared to take the issue very seriously.

"He asked me to take my jacket off," said Glick, who had been bare chested under the denim prospect jacket he was wearing. "Then he took a tool I had in my bag, kind of like a wire cutter, and put it over one of my nipples."

What followed was a drunken test of nerve, Glick said.

"What would you think if I cut this off?" the biker boss asked as he put pressure on Glick's nipple with the wire cutter.

"It's not something I need," Glick answered.

There was a moment when both men stared into each other's eyes; then the biker boss laughed, and everyone who was watching joined in. Glick kept his nipple that night and exchanged his prospect jacket for full Pagan colors. It was a seminal event in his life as a biker and one that he still recounts with a combination of pride and regret.

Pride in what he had become. Regret because he can no longer be a part of that world.

Drugs and booze took up the rest of that night. Glick said he crashed in one of the motel rooms with two other bikers. Around three in the morning, there was a knock on the door.

"It was a hooker," he said with a laugh. "She was working the party. She offered to give all three of us blow jobs, fifteen dollars each. I had just been inducted into the club, so I thought I should pay. I negotiated the deal. Forty bucks for all three of us."

It was good to be a Pagan.

Two years later, Glick would memorialize his membership at a tattoo parlor where an artist would cover his right arm, from shoulder to elbow, in the outlaw biker gang's code and colors. Across the top of the tattoo in blue ink was the word "Pagan's." At the bottom were the initials "MC" for "motorcycle club." A diamond outlined in red and mounted on a burning cross formed the center of the artwork. On the right side of the diamond were the letters "LPDP"—Live a Pagan, Die a Pagan. Down the left side were "PFFP"—Pagan Forever, Forever Pagan. And in the middle of the diamond was "1%."

While Augello was clearly his early mentor, the guy Glick most respected, and the one he still talks about with some admiration, was John Kachbalian, an Atlantic County biker and former Pagan known as "the Egyptian." Kachbalian did time in the 1980s after being convicted with several other club members in a racketeering case built around drug dealing. The key witness in that federal investigation was James "Jimmy D" De-Gregorio, a onetime "cooker" for the Pagans. DeGregorio, who went on to write a book about his biker days, began cooperating after being arrested for kidnapping and shooting a ranking member of the Philadelphia Mafia in a dispute over the meth business. As a cooker, DeGregorio did the chemical work required to produce meth in hidden biker labs. His product, known as "Pagan Purple," was considered of the highest quality.

Kachbalian was one of nearly two dozen Pagans indicted in a massive RICO case that focused on Pagans and the methamphetamine trade. At the time of his arrest in 1984, Kachbalian was just twenty-two years old but was the president of the Philadelphia chapter of the Pagans.

He was sentenced to fifteen years in prison. He served about twelve. After his release, he relocated to Atlantic County and started his own construction business. Sometimes described as a "retired" or "former" Pagan, Kachbalian was regarded as a veteran biker by club members like Glick.

"I met him when I was riding with the Tribe [a Pagans support club] in 2004," Glick said. "We became friends after I was initiated. He taught me a lot. I respected him. He believed in the brotherhood, and he was a stickler for the rules. A lot of guys didn't like him for that reason, but I respected him for that. And when I got the diamond [the presidency of a chapter] I tried to operate the way he would."

Kachbalian was always ready to help, to offer advice and counsel. This was especially true when Glick started to sour on some of the petty, backbiting club intrigue that is a common but seldom discussed part of the biker underworld.

"He wouldn't admit it now, but I think he thought he was passing the torch to me," Glick said. "I think we both felt the same way about what it meant to be a Pagan."

While most members paid lip service to the concepts of loyalty and brotherhood that were at the core of the outlaw biker code, Glick said many bikers were only interested in the money and power that being in the club might bring. In some ways, an outlaw biker gang is like a Mafia family. Both are highly structured. Both are governed by sets of rules and codes of conduct. And both tout the exclusivity of membership.

But like many twenty-first-century mafiosi, many bikers have lost sight of what being in a club is supposed to mean. Honor and loyalty have been replaced by greed and treachery. Guys get involved not because they see membership as a way of life, but because they see it as a way to make money.

Freddy Augello was one example, but there were others.

Glick said that early in his tenure as Cape May County chapter president, he balked at a New Jersey Mother Club leader who insisted that members from throughout the state meet monthly at a bar in Elizabeth, where he was headquartered.

"I found out this guy was living rent free in an apartment above the bar as long as he brought customers in," Glick said. "That was the reason for the meetings, to make money for the bar owner."

Glick said he complained and then said if his chapter was required to attend, they would bring their own beer.

"I joined the Pagans to extort people, not to be extorted," he said.

There was another incident, at the Roar to the Shore in Wildwood, in which a chapter president from central New Jersey was brutally beaten because he had been forcing members and their women to engage in sex parties.

"If someone wants to do that, it's fine," Glick said. "But you can't force somebody if they don't want to do it. Turned out the guy who got beaten wasn't doing that at all, but his vice president wanted to take over, and he lied about it."

Internal politics that had little to do with the rules of the biker underworld were always in play. Glick said he moved from the Cape May chapter to the Atlantic County chapter of the Pagans after he was criticized for refusing to buy his meth from a Pagan.

"I had my own source," Glick said. "And what I got and what I sold was pure, high quality. They wanted me to buy meth that had been diluted. It wasn't as good. I wouldn't do it."

Glick said he gave up his diamond in protest and switched his affiliation to the Atlantic County chapter of the Pagans. Within months he was elevated to the rank of president and had the diamond again. But the bickering and pettiness continued. In some ways, he said, it was like the sophomoric backstabbing that you might find in a college fraternity. The only difference was the potential for real violence.

Kachbalian, he said, told him to have patience and not to overreact. To look at the long game. Kachbalian himself had problems at one time and was asked to turn in his colors. Glick said he refused.

"Two guys from the Mother Club came down to see him," said Glick. Kachbalian owned a small construction company at the time.

"He was a great carpenter, meticulous," Glick said. "He could do anything. And he was tough. He fell off a ladder one time while working on a roof. Two stories. Got busted up pretty bad. But for three weeks, he continued to ride his bike. His wife finally made him go to the doctor. He had a broken back."

The Mother Club members told Kachbalian they were there to take his jacket, his colors, according to Glick, who said the Egyptian later told him the story.

"This is a guy who had done twelve years [in prison] for the club, and now they want his colors? They're in his garage. He looks around and grabs two pipes. He hands one to each of these guys, and then he picks one up himself."

The bikers were puzzled.

"He tells them, 'I don't want you to say you didn't have anything to protect yourselves.' They backed off and left without his colors. That's the kind of guy he is. Fearless and full of respect for the club. That same night he calls me up and says he needs some of the 'jewelry' I was holding for him. He meant he needed a gun. I brought one right over to him. He didn't know if those guys would be coming back, and he wanted to be ready."

Too often, Glick said, the leadership of the organization applied the rules only when it benefited themselves. A North Jersey support club, for example, had three members who had once worked in law enforcement. Yet they were allowed to wear "P-patches" on their jackets, signifying they belonged to a Pagan support club.

"That's against the rules," Glick said. "No one in law enforcement and no former law enforcement official can be part of anything associated with us. But these guys were apparently paying the local club, so that was okay. I made it an issue. It wasn't right. I think I pissed some people off. But why have rules if you don't abide by them?"

Another North Jersey member was forced out, Glick said, because his girlfriend had been arrested in a minor drug case and ended up giving a statement to the New Jersey State Police about the gang.

"She didn't really give up much, but it created a problem," Glick said. "She shouldn't have done it."

Her biker boyfriend was told he couldn't see her anymore.

"He was forty-eight. She was twenty-five," Glick said. "They had just had a baby. He was told he had to give her and the baby up. He wouldn't do it."

So he was forced out of the club.

Glick had another go-round with the Mother Club in 2016 after he was asked to intercede in a dispute involving an Atlantic County club member. The member, a Vietnam vet who had been riding with the Pagans for nineteen years, was asked to turn in his colors because he wasn't showing up for regular meetings.

Glick didn't like the guy, thought he was arrogant. But since he was president of the Atlantic County chapter at the time, Glick said he met with the vet and offered to help. The vet said he had gotten permission to "retire" from some former Mother Club leaders. Retirees didn't have to attend meetings.

"But the new [Mother Club] administration didn't accept that," Glick said. "It was all politics. He had been close to some older guys who weren't in charge anymore. The new guys wanted his jacket."

Politics of the more traditional sort would also have an impact on Glick at this time. In June of 2016, Jim McClain, the Atlantic County prosecutor, was nominated as a state superior court judge by Governor Chris Christie. The nomination was quickly confirmed by the state legislature, and McClain donned the robe of a superior court judge assigned to the state civil court bench in Atlantic City. His first assistant prosecutor, Diane Ruberton, was tapped to serve as acting prosecutor, with the presumption in many Republican political circles that the governor would eventually make her appointment permanent.

That never happened.

Instead, in February of 2017, Christie, a Republican, nominated Damon Tyner, a Democrat, as the prosecutor of Atlantic County. Tyner had twice sought election to the New Jersey State Assembly from Atlantic County as a Democrat. He had lost both races. He was then appointed as a superior court judge and assigned to a bench in family court, where he had been serving since 2014.

That a Republican governor would nominate a Democrat to the highest law enforcement post in a borderline Republican county raised eyebrows in some political circles. Others, however, saw it as a pragmatic political move by Christie, who knew how the game was played in New Jersey. Christie had once been the US attorney for New Jersey, the highest law enforcement official in the state. During his time as a prosecutor and even later when he became governor, he had had a political relationship—some might call it an alliance—with George Norcross, the powerful Democratic political boss of South Jersey.

Tyner's appointment as county prosecutor, many believe, was arranged by Norcross. It was Tyner's reward for running for the state assembly in what was then a heavily Republican district. Needless to say, the odd man—or woman—out was Diane Ruberton, who was bumped back down to a first assistant prosecutor's position. She would be heard from again, but that's getting ahead of the story.

One of the first things Damon Tyner did after taking office early in 2017 was refocus on the April Kauffman investigation.

TEN

Maybe it was a coincidence.

Maybe it was paranoia.

But shortly after Tyner was appointed prosecutor and pushed his investigators to focus on the April Kauffman murder, James Kauffman went ballistic. This was during a visit Freddy's ex-wife, Beverly, made to the doctor's office.

Beverly had replaced Glenn Seeler as a conduit for messages between her ex-husband and the doctor. While she and Freddy had separated around 2003 and had divorced five years later, they still saw each other on a regular basis because they worked together in the sign-painting company that Freddy owned. She did some of the artwork.

She also had become part of the pill mill operation early on. Injured in a car accident, she had a legitimate medical need for pain pills. But she had no medical insurance. James Kauffman wrote her scripts for oxycodone on a regular basis. She kept some of the pills for her personal use and gave the rest to Fred, who sold them.

During a visit early in 2017, Beverly Augello got more than a script when she visited James Kauffman's office. The doctor went on a rant about the Pagans and the police. After leaving the office, she told Fred that the doctor was "freaking out," claiming someone in the biker underworld was cooperating with authorities.

Augello called Glick and told him to get over to the doctor's office as soon as possible and find out what was going on. He also said that he wanted to meet with the doctor face-to-face, and he wasn't going to take no for an answer. Glick called the office and made up a story. He said he thought he had an infected toe and needed to see the doc right away. This would be consistent with a patient being treated for diabetes, as Glick was. When he got there, the doctor was still riled up.

"He said one of his lawyers had heard that a Pagan had been arrested and was cooperating," Glick recalled. "We didn't know anything about that, but I told him we would check it out."

There is a communications network within the biker underworld. The leaders of different chapters contact one another on a regular basis. They might want to check out a recruit and ask if anyone knows the guy or any reason he shouldn't be trusted. They might have word about an undercover law enforcement agent or a cooperator working the area, or about a pending drug bust or, on a positive note from the biker perspective, about an opportunity to make some money or score some drugs or to party with some willing go-go dancers who are looking to turn tricks.

In this case, Glick and Augello wanted to know if any Pagan had been arrested. That kind of information is readily available. If a member is pinched, his chapter knows about it. Phone calls and messages went out. The word that came back was that no one was in jail; no one had been charged with any crime. Kauffman's information was bogus, maybe part of his growing paranoia or maybe part of a disinformation campaign that authorities were using to stir the pot. No one was in custody; no biker was giving up any information about the murder. But the issue set Glick's mind working again. The murder investigation had been going on for almost five years. It was hard to believe that no one had made the connection between the doctor and the bikers.

Whether Beverly Augello had those same concerns is a matter of conjecture. What is certain is that around this time she decided to get out of town, to leave her past behind, to get a fresh start. Like Glenn Seeler and Cheryl Pizza, she headed south, relocating to Summerland Key, Florida, about twenty miles east of Key West. That was where she was living when she was arrested in the pill mill case.

The past that she was running from included her marriage to Augello when she was twenty-seven. Freddy was forty-two at the time and a major figure in the Pagans. She became his "old lady," a biker designation that might be a slight step above the "property of" identifier often attached to women. Both indicated that the woman belonged to the biker who had claimed her. The "old lady" designation was considered somewhat more permanent, and the woman was less likely to be shared sexually with any other members of the club. Beverly Augello's biker experience wasn't the only part of her past that she hoped to leave behind.

Authorities had learned that she was one of the patients James Kauffman saw on the morning of May 10, 2012. They would also learn—and she would later confirm—that on that morning, while at the doctor's office, she was given an envelope to take to Fred Augello. She said she had no idea what the envelope contained and never looked inside.

Investigators believe it was the final cash payment for the murder that had been carried out that morning. James Kauffman would be the grieving husband vomiting on his front lawn after he arrived at his home in Linwood later that day and discovered his wife dead, but first he had to pay for the shooting that left her sprawled on their bedroom floor.

How Kauffman was reacting to the mounting pressure and whether he would "stand up" if pressed by authorities was what Fred Augello wanted to find out. And he figured the only way to do this was to meet the doctor in person. That was what Glick tried to set up during that meeting in the doc's office.

"I said, 'Look, we're not taking no for an answer. You got to meet with him, and he wants it soon.' The doc said he'd call me by the end of the week."

Glick said he had met with Kauffman on a Wednesday. By Friday, he said, he still had not heard from the doctor.

"The doc blew it off for about a week," he said. "Fred was getting more upset. I was annoyed because the doc was telling me he would meet, but would never call to confirm it. He blew us off for eight days. Then he called me. He said, 'Tell Hollywood tomorrow, noon, at the ShopRite.' The ShopRite was right down the street from his office. They were going to meet in the parking lot."

After the meeting, Augello had some disturbing news for Glick. He said the doctor wanted "a gun that couldn't be traced."

"Freddy said the doc offered to knock off his fee for two scripts—a thousand dollars—if we could get him the gun," Glick said. "He also said the doctor complained about Kim Pack, April's daughter. 'Everything would be fine if that fuckin' bitch would just let it rest,' he said the doctor told him."

James Kauffman had said much the same thing to Glick during several of his visits to the doctor's office. Kauffman, he said, would whine about Pack and about several of April's friends who were constantly agitating about the stalled investigation.

"He used to complain about [one of April's] best friends, about how she don't give it up, said she was a 'persistent bitch,'" Glick said. "I would be like, 'How ya doin'?' and he would say, 'I'd be fine if that fucking bitch just stopped.'"

Every May, on the anniversary of the murder, there would be articles and news reports in which Kim Pack and several of April's close friends would be quoted. It was apparently getting to James Kauffman.

Glick said the doc told him they "ain't never gonna let this rest."

Glick said he would feign sympathy but would jokingly add, "I'm pretty sure there's no statute [of limitations]" in a murder case, meaning the investigation would never really go away.

"But I'm innocent," he said the doctor would reply.

Glick said he would just nod his head in seeming agreement. The doctor, he said, was in denial.

To placate him, Augello and Glick said they would try to find a gun that couldn't be traced. But they had no intention of doing so, Glick added.

Why Kauffman wanted a gun and what he intended to do with it have never been determined. But he was right to be concerned about the ramped-up investigation. For the first time since the murder of her mother, it appeared Kim Pack had someone in the prosecutor's office willing to listen to what she and her attorney had uncovered. More important, they had someone who was willing to act.

Andrew Glick was on his way to work on June 13, 2017, at around seven o'clock in the morning. His route to the senior citizen facility where he was the executive chef took him past James Kauffman's suite of offices on Ocean Heights Avenue in Egg Harbor Township. That morning, as Glick drove by, he saw a half dozen law enforcement vehicles—cars and SUVs—parked strategically around the building. He also saw more than a dozen cops, many wearing bulletproof vests, their weapons drawn, taking cover behind those vehicles and focusing on the front door of James Kauffman's office.

It had taken more than five years, Glick thought as he drove by, but authorities had finally come knocking on the door. How soon, he wondered, would they be at his?

"I got to work that day, and it was like I was sleepwalking," Glick recalled. "I kept wondering how soon it would be before they were at my house. Finally, I went to my boss and told him I was sick. I had to go home."

Glick's mind was going a mile a minute as he drove back past the doctor's office. The parking lot was still full of police vehicles. As he drove, he was doing an inventory of the product, cash and weapons he had in his house. He knew he had to get everything out of there. It would just be a matter of time, he figured, before the guys in the bulletproof vests would be coming for him.

"I rented a storage facility," he said. "It cost like a hundred bucks a month. And I moved everything there."

"Everything" included meth, cocaine, cash and weapons. Glick had several rifles and handguns. All had been purchased legitimately. But he didn't want to take any chances. He knew if there was a raid, the cops would scoop everything up.

He was right about that. And he was also right to believe that there would be a raid on his home. But that wouldn't take place until later in the year. At this point, with news breaking about the raid on Kauffman's office, all he and Freddy Augello could do was watch and wonder.

The raid began at six forty a.m., shortly after James Kauffman arrived at his office and before any of his staff had reported for work. That, of course, was the plan. Investigators knew Kauffman's work routine and staged the raid around it.

Detective James Scoppa Jr. and FBI agent Daniel Garrabrant, who headed the medical insurance–fraud probe, had coordinated the move. Other agents and investigators from the FBI, the prosecutor's office and the Linwood and Egg Harbor Township police departments were also on the scene that morning.

The events were recorded in real time by body cameras worn by some of the police officials on hand. (The video can still be viewed online.) The raid did not go off smoothly. James Kauffman, dressed in scrubs, answered a knock on the office door by Scoppa, who said he was there to serve a warrant. Kauffman quickly shut the door, shouting, "I'm going to kill myself!"

He returned seconds later, brandishing a Ruger 9mm handgun.

"I'm not going to jail for this," he said. "I'm going to kill myself."

Scoppa pleaded with Kauffman to put down the gun. Other officers and agents took up positions behind their vehicles, weapons drawn. Scoppa told the doctor the search warrant was part of a medical insurance–fraud investigation.

"Drop the gun!" Scoppa and other officers shouted. "Drop the gun! We have a search warrant. . . . Drop the gun! Drop the gun! Let's talk. . . . You are not under arrest."

"Bullshit. I don't believe it," Kauffman said, apparently convinced that the police were there to arrest him for the murder of his wife. About a month earlier, in fact, the Atlantic County Prosecutor's Office had sought a DNA sample from the doctor—a request that he was legally challenging but one that seemed to indicate the murder probe was heating up.

Kauffman stood in the vestibule of his office, behind two glass doors, then returned to his office, closing the door behind him. A few minutes later, he came out again, still carrying the gun and threatening to kill himself.

Scoppa had thrown the search warrant toward the doors of the office vestibule. The warrant fluttered through the air and separated, pages landing in the bushes and dark mulch of the neatly manicured lawn that surrounded the office building.

"This is just a search warrant for medical stuff," shouted FBI agent Daniel Garrabrant. "You're not going to jail."

"I don't believe you," Kauffman said as he quickly gathered up the search warrant papers and headed back into his office.

Law enforcement officers quickly fanned out around the building, moving their cars and SUVs to strategic locations.

The body cameras and recorders picked up some of the activity.

"We have one at gunpoint," one officer was heard saying as he called in for more backup. "Dr. James Kauffman. He has a weapon."

The raid played out on a warm, bright spring morning. Periodically, the body cameras picking up the video and audio would include the sounds of birds chirping.

During what would amount to a forty-minute standoff, the doctor could be seen moving through the suite of rooms that made up his office. He appeared agitated. The officers outside continued to communicate with one another and with new law enforcement arrivals.

"We have a barricaded suspect inside," came the report over one law enforcement audio transmitter. "He has a gun."

A hostage negotiator was called in and, via telephone, began talking to the doctor, trying to convince him that he was overreacting, that this was merely a medical insurance–fraud investigation, that the search warrant was for medical records, that there was no reason for guns and no need for violence.

Carole Weintraub was lying in bed that morning in her Philadelphia condo when the phone rang. She was expecting the call. Jimmy would phone her every morning to say hello and let her know he had gotten to work as usual.

This morning was no different, but she noticed something in his voice.

"I just want you to know that I love you," he said.

"I love you too," Carole said. "What's going on?"

"I just have to go," he said. Then he hung up.

Carole tried calling him back but there was no answer.

A short time later, her phone rang again. This time it was the law office of Edwin Jacobs. One of Jacobs's assistants told Carole that there was a standoff in progress at her husband's office and that police were trying to get him to come out and surrender.

James Kauffman eventually did just that. He walked out of his office at seven eighteen, leaving his gun behind. He was told to turn around and walk backward toward one of the police vans. In the shade of a cluster of trees that lined the office parking lot, he was handcuffed. Authorities thanked him for taking the calls from the negotiator. He complained about his bad shoulder.

"Now what happens?" he asked.

Authorities said they were going to search his office and asked about the location of various records and keys to open any drawers, safes or filing cabinets. Kauffman politely provided answers and directions and apologized for keeping a "messy desk."

He also said the basement was "a mess. . . . Again, I apologize."

There were search warrants, he was told, for his office, his home, his vehicle and his cell phone.

"But they've searched it all before," he said.

When he was asked about his gun, he said it was in the office, adding, "It's a legal weapon."

And when they took his cell phone, he cautioned, "My whole

life is on that phone." Ever cooperative, he then offered the password to open the phone—"GLANDS69," he said.

He asked if he would get his car back and was told he would.

"Like, today?" he asked.

"We'll see how it goes," one of the investigators said.

As it would turn out, James Kauffman would never again have the need for a car. Although he and those who supported him didn't know it at the time, as he was placed under arrest and walked to an ambulance that would drive him to a nearby hospital, James Kauffman's days of freedom had ended. He would spend the rest of his life living in a jail cell.

Before he was taken to the ambulance, he was told by an FBI agent that he would receive an itemized list of everything that was taken during the executions of the search warrants.

"I appreciate it, sir," he replied.

He then asked why he was being taken to a hospital.

"Sir, because you threatened suicide," a detective said.

"Oh, cut me a break," Kauffman replied. "I'm really fine."

Situated in the back of an ambulance, James Kauffman was driven that morning to the psychiatric unit at AtlantiCare Regional Medical Center. Later, he was charged with unlawful possession of a weapon, possession of hollow-point bullets and obstruction of justice.

After a court hearing where bail was denied, Edwin Jacobs told reporters that his client was under intense pressure because he'd been subjected to a "relentless five-year investigation focusing on nobody else."

When Carole heard about the police standoff and her husband's arrest, "I literally didn't know what to do," she said. "I was paralyzed. I didn't know what phone calls to make. This was uncharted territory. Let alone being totally shocked by the situation itself. My husband is incarcerated."

So Carole picked up her cell phone and called an old friend of hers, somebody she knew would be cool under fire.

Jennifer Cooper was a veteran commercial airline pilot who that morning was scheduled to fly out of Newark Airport. But when Jennifer heard what was going on—"Jim has been arrested," Carole told her—Cooper made a snap decision. She told her boss, "I can't fly; I'm not fit for duty."

Jennifer's mind was locked on her friend and the unfolding drama down the Jersey Shore starring James Kauffman.

Oh my God, Jennifer thought to herself. *I need to be with Carole. There's nobody else there. . . . She needs to be supported.*

Jennifer and her husband, another pilot, had been out to dinner quite a few times with Carole and Jim. The Kauffmans had also been dinner guests at Jennifer's house.

"I liked Jim," Jennifer said. "I felt he really knew his profession, really knew his job. He was a little cocky," she admitted, but she excused that by saying that Dr. Kauffman reminded her of "one of those cocky pilots" she knew too well.

But he "was always very personable, very nice, and fun to be with," Jennifer said. "A good conversationalist."

And Carole was one of her oldest and dearest friends.

Jennifer called Carole back and said two words: "I'm coming."

"You don't have to," Carole told her.

"Yes, I do," Jennifer said. "I can handle it."

They agreed to rendezvous at the AtlantiCare Regional

Medical Center, where Kauffman was supposed to be undergoing a psychiatric exam. At the hospital, however, the staff told Carole that she wasn't going to be allowed to see her husband, who, after the exam, was on his way to prison.

"Carole was still in shock. She was numb," Jennifer recalled. "She kept saying, 'He is so stupid' and 'I can't believe this is happening.'"

Carole's next stop was the lockup at the Linwood Police Department, but James Kauffman wasn't there. He was being held at the Atlantic County Jail, his lawyer told Carole. But when Carole got to the jail and asked to see her husband, she got the runaround from one prison official after another. Finally, she was told she would have to come back on Saturday. The jail had visiting hours only on weekends. This was a Tuesday.

"She was furious at the incompetency," Jennifer recalled. She was fuming. As far as Cooper was concerned, the authorities seemed intent on punishing James Kauffman, whom they had long suspected of murdering his wife.

As they sat in Carole's car and pondered what to do next, Jennifer's cell phone rang. More bad news. Jennifer's mother, who lived in Chicago, had just suffered a stroke. Carole drove Jennifer back to the Linwood Police Station, where Jennifer had left her car. Jennifer then drove to Philadelphia, where she caught a plane to Chicago.

Carole didn't see her husband for three weeks. But what she did see, over and over again, was the body cam video of his arrest, which was splashed all over TV news and the Internet.

Her first reaction was "You stupid jackass, how could you be so stupid?"

"It was like watching a train wreck. You hate what you see, but you can't look away," she said. "To me it was revolting. Maybe this is unkind, but I thought he was stupid to even think about waving a gun."

Carole's daughter, Abby, however, was thrilled to hear the news that Kauffman had just gotten arrested. "They got him," she yelled to everybody at the store where she worked as a cashier. And when she watched the body cam video, she thought it was proof that the man her mother had married was "psycho, bat-shit crazy."

Atlantic County prosecutor Damon Tyner was coy when asked by reporters if the raid had had anything to do with the ongoing investigation into the death of April Kauffman.

"No, but yes," he told reporters, according to a news account in the *Press of Atlantic City*. Tyner made the comment during a news conference outside the doctor's office shortly after the raid, the paper reported. He emphasized that the arrest was the result of the doctor's actions that morning and not part of the murder probe.

"He brandished a weapon and pointed it at law enforcement officers," Tyner said. "He was very adamant that he did not want to be served with any type of papers."

Tyner had been in office about three months and he had clearly changed the way the game was being played. While his predecessor, James McClain, had said very little publicly about the murder case, Tyner seemed to take every opportunity he could to focus media attention on the investigation.

While others in law enforcement might have shied away from the cameras, Tyner seemed to enjoy standing in the spotlight.

"We sometimes had to rein him in," a former judicial associate said of Tyner's penchant for bold statements and media attention while he served as a judge.

Another, more critical assessment, came from an attorney who had watched Tyner in action both as an attorney and as a judge. "He's a knucklehead," the lawyer said.

Tyner's late father, Henry, had been a high-profile and well-regarded Atlantic City police inspector who later became a city councilman. He was frequently quoted in news accounts both while investigating major crimes and while serving on the city council. Damon Tyner grew up watching his father deal with and benefit from positive media attention. As county prosecutor, he was following in his dad's law enforcement footsteps. The same could be said for his approach to dealing with the media.

"No comment," the standard phrase from many in law enforcement, was not a typical response in the Tyner (father and son) media playbook.

Damon Tyner had made it clear from the moment he was appointed earlier in the year that solving the April Kauffman homicide would be a top priority of his office. That investigation, he told reporters, was "ongoing" and "widespread."

While he had said little about the murder investigation while talking to reporters outside Kauffman's office after the raid, in a separate news briefing at his own office that day he told reporters that the April Kauffman case "is very important to her family and to the community. Though the case has been rather quiet for the past five years, it is a very active case. Every day that passes, we learn more as more people remember things, and I hope that I will be able to bring some peace and some closure to this family and this community."

Tyner's office had successfully argued that James Kauffman should not be granted bail while he awaited trial on the weapons and obstruction-of-justice charges. He was, authorities argued, a potential danger to the community. He might also be a flight risk.

Pressure was beginning to build on all those around James Kauffman, including his wife, Carole.

On June 16, three days after the raid, Carole was alone in her condo, watching Chris Matthews on MSNBC. Shortly after seven p.m., she heard a knock on the door. It was the building engineer, with three cops standing behind him.

"They're here to see you," he said. One of the men, Detective Scoppa, stepped in front and told her he had a search warrant for her apartment.

"Why?" she asked.

They were searching all of the properties that James Kauffman's name was on, he explained. It was part of a federal investigation into the compound-cream scam.

"Have at it," Carole said. "Come on in."

The investigators were looking for cash and guns. They found both. Jimmy had always kept a lot of cash around; so had Carole. She was always worried about her luck running out. She had a fear of winding up as a bag lady. But during the search, Carole began to realize that she had more to lose than her cash. She overheard the cops talking about seizing her condo. Although Carole had put her husband's name on the deed, when she bought the place on February 10, 2016, it was with $1,350,000 of her own money. "I have a paper trail," she told the cops, referring to the personal accounts from which the money had come to make the purchase.

What was more, it angered her when she thought that these investigators, who knew nothing about her, never even considered that she had had her own life, money and career before she reconnected with James Kauffman.

"I've worked since I was twelve years old," she said. "I always had a job. I babysat. I worked every summer. I came out of college debt free, thanks to my parents, but I worked for everything I got. My parents gave me a start, but I never borrowed anything."

During the search, investigators found a gun that Carole didn't know was in the house. She asked them to disassemble it. They also talked about the compound-cream scam that involved police, firemen and teachers in Jersey Shore communities and how their health insurer had been ripped off, paying out millions in insurance claims for $10,000 tubes of medication that cost as little as ten dollars to produce. Investigators, she realized, were convinced that she had been a conduit for Jimmy, that he was using her to launder some of his profits from the insurance scam.

"We've got you now," she said Scoppa told her.

The search of the condo took nearly four hours. Carole was forced to stand outside in the hallway. She eventually went downstairs and sat in the building engineer's office. At one point, she got so worked up about what was going on that she passed out and wound up lying on the floor.

"They literally had to pick me up," she said. She couldn't

believe that the police were searching her house and that she was now trapped in Jimmy's messy life. "They went through everything. . . . No reasonable thought was going through my head."

After the cops left, Carole moved to protect her condo from seizure. She gathered copies of withdrawals she had made from her Vanguard account and subsequently deposited into her checking account to prove that she alone had paid for her condo. She gave those financial records to her lawyers, who shared them with prosecutors.

It was the last Carole ever heard about any threat to seize her condo. She had put her husband's name on the deed only as a courtesy, she said, because she wanted him to know she was willing to share whatever assets she had in their new marriage. At the time, she said, her husband was in no shape to help her out financially, as he was drowning in debts of between $600,000 and $700,000. That was why "not a dime" toward the purchase of the condo came from him, Carole said.

In retrospect, Carole realized it had been a dumb move to put Jimmy's name on anything with all the trouble he was involved in. "I was a jackass," she said.

Carole was able to save her condo from seizure. But since she couldn't prove whose cash was in the condo, she had no chance to get back the $68,407 that the cops had seized when they searched her place. The cash would never be recovered. It was something she planned to discuss with her husband when she finally got to see him. It was only part of what his troubles cost her.

There was a lot Carole wanted to say to Jimmy, but in the

short term, she was unable to visit him. He was being held in solitary confinement in the Atlantic County Jail.

Reactions to his arrest varied. Abby, her daughter, was gleeful. She said if she had had a chance to visit her stepfather in jail, she would have told him, "You're exactly where you belong."

That sentiment, in all probability, was shared by Kim Pack, Kauffman's other stepdaughter. While Abby and Kim have never met, it was astonishing how similar their views and perceptions of James Kauffman were. He had dealt with both of them in the same cold, heartless way. And they both were happy to see him behind bars.

But Carole also heard words of encouragement and support.

"Dear Dr. Kauffman," read a note sent from a patient. "Just a little note to say prayers and thoughts are with you and your family. After 19 years of knowing you I consider you a friend. Hope to see you again."

"Thank you from the bottom of my heart for taking such good care of me all these years," wrote another patient. "You will really be missed. God bless you."

"Thanks for literally saving my life with the hyperthyroidism diagnosis," wrote a third. "You're the best. Stay strong and patient. Praying for your speedy release."

There would be no release.

Instead, as James Kauffman tried to adjust to life behind bars, Carole Weintraub began to reassess just who her husband was, what he had done and what the future might hold.

Freddy Augello had the same questions and concerns. And within days of the June 13 raid, he began to pressure Andrew

Glick for the answers. They met at the Cheese Board, a local restaurant.

"I had a soda; he's eating a sandwich," Glick said. "He says he just wants to get my opinion on what do I think . . . happened and do we think it's about our thing or is it something else?

"'What can we do?'" Glick said Augello asked, and then wondered if Glick had anybody "on the inside."

Glick shook his head, amazed at the question.

"I really don't have a lot of cop friends, ya know," he said.

He suggested that Augello do what he had already done—clean up his house and his office, removing anything that might link him to a crime, anything the police could use to bring pressure.

Five years after the murder, Augello and Glick were finally accepting the fact that it was no longer a question of if the police were coming, but rather a question of when.

ELEVEN

S hortly after the raid, authorities announced that patients who needed their medical records could retrieve them by contacting the Atlantic County Prosecutor's Office.

Andrew Glick figured the smart move was to ask for his. He was being treated for diabetes, so his visits to Kauffman's office were "legitimate." Not to ask for the records, he reasoned, might have aroused suspicion. In addition, he wanted to see what authorities would say when he turned up.

So about three weeks after James Kauffman was arrested, Andrew Glick was sitting in the Atlantic County Prosecutor's Office in Mays Landing, talking with the detective who had led the raid and a lieutenant who was also working the case. They would be happy to turn over his medical records, they said, but first they had a few questions.

And that was when the idea of cooperating was first put on the table.

Detective Scoppa told Glick that they knew all about the pill mill operation and the murder for hire. It was just a matter of time, he said, before Kauffman and those involved in the homicide would be facing murder and conspiracy charges. The raid and Kauffman's arrest in the medical insurance–fraud case was just the first step. There was more to come.

Glick was told that now was his chance to help himself.

It was the typical law enforcement offer, one that potential cooperators hear every day in prosecutors' offices all over the country. Authorities use various analogies to make the point, but the pitch goes something like this: the train is leaving the station. There are only so many seats left. Now's the time to get on board. If some of your fellow conspirators decide to make the move, there may not be room for you on the train. More important, we may not need you. If that happens, you'll be sitting at the defense table, looking at life in prison, instead of sitting in the witness stand, coming clean. It's your decision. Help yourself. Do it now before it's too late.

Glick got a version of that pitch from Scoppa, who said the murder would be solved, people would be charged and those involved, even if they hadn't actually pulled the trigger, would be facing twenty years for a murder conspiracy rap.

But the detective told him, "If you had no involvement in her death, but just received the offer, you couldn't legally be charged with conspiracy."

That was the carrot authorities dangled in front of Andrew Glick: tell us what you know, and we'll work something out.

Glick, who spent several hours with authorities that day, said he wanted to speak with his lawyer. A call was put in to the attorney, who had a court appearance in North Jersey. He wouldn't be back until later. Glick and his interrogators waited.

When the lawyer finally arrived, preliminary negotiations began. But no deal was struck. Glick wasn't ready to give it all up. So he took his medical records and went home. He said his lawyer continued to talk with investigators that summer. Nothing was agreed upon, and in September, Glick told him he wasn't interested in cooperating. The talks were discontinued, but Glick said he told his lawyer, "I could possibly have all the information to solve the biggest case in Atlantic County in the last twenty years." He said he had some "firsthand" information about the murder plot, but nothing "up close and personal" about the actual shooting. He said he knew just about everything that had happened, but didn't know where the gun was.

"I pretty much know where the money came from and who hired who," he told his lawyer.

"That's a lot to know," his lawyer replied.

And all of it would figure in the ongoing investigation.

Glick told Fred Augello about what the detective had said but withheld the part about his lawyer entertaining a cooperation agreement. The smartest course of action, he figured, was to acknowledge he had been questioned, so he told Augello that when he went to pick up his medical records, he had been "detained" by Scoppa. That way if a rumor later circulated (and if nothing else, the murder case was rife with rumors), Glick had covered his ass. Sure, he had been questioned. But he hadn't given anything up.

That part, at least, was true.

"Fred wanted to know everything," he said. "He was worried that the doc would give us all up. I didn't think that was likely. The doc was in the middle of the murder plot. He was the one who made it happen. But Freddy thought he might try to work something out, that they would offer him a deal like in the Hannibal Lecter movie—you'll never get out of prison, but tell us what we want to know, and we'll make sure you spend the rest of your life in a decent facility with a nice view."

Even though he knew Glick was aware of most of the details, Augello still talked in vague terms about the murder plot, who was involved and who had done what, Glick said. When he asked about the murder weapon, he said Augello told him, "It's gone, never to be found."

Augello's concern about someone cooperating was a topic he would come back to again and again in conversations with Glick over the next six months. Ironically, the person he was talking to was the man who investigators had already decided could help them break the case wide open.

Glick tried to focus on everyday life, to go about his business in as normal a way as possible. But normal wasn't happening that summer. His girlfriend, a woman who was in an abusive relationship with the father of her two young children, needed a place to stay. Andrew Glick brought her and her two young children home to live with him and his wife.

At first, his wife, who knew the woman socially, accepted the story that he was just helping a friend who needed to get away from a man who beat her up. But his wife grew more and more suspicious as the summer wore on.

"My girlfriend could dress provocatively sometimes," he said. "And my wife started to notice that just before I would get home from work, she would change into something nice."

Glick said he and his girlfriend would often stay up late to watch television after her kids and his wife had gone to bed, and that on at least two occasions she nearly caught them making love on a couch. The situation at home was getting as tense as the murder investigation.

The Atlantic County Jail, officially the Gerald L. Gormley Justice Facility, is located in a wooded area in Mays Landing, about a half mile from the criminal courthouse complex. Opened in 1985 and originally designed to house about four hundred inmates, the jail has been expanded several times and now is home to about a thousand prisoners, both male and female. Most are awaiting trial or serving short (a year or less) prison sentences. Fencing, wiring and high-tech surveillance equipment are part of an extensive security system. For the past three years, 2017 through 2019, state inspectors have recognized the jail as being 100 percent in compliance with state codes and regulations. The state inspection looks at such issues as training and staff development, sanitation, disciplinary procedures, security, and food, inmate and health services.

Visiting hours at the jail are limited to weekends. Hours on both Saturday and Sunday are ten a.m. to nine p.m. for prisoners in general population and nine a.m. to ten a.m. for those in high security.

Carole Weintraub had never been inside a jail before. It

wasn't a pleasant experience. And while state inspectors might have given the jail their seal of approval, when she finally got into the facility to see her husband, she was shocked by what she saw.

"It's dirty, it's inhumane, it's awful," she said.

Especially the bathrooms. Carole took pictures with her iPhone of stained sinks, toilets surrounded by used toilet paper and paper towels and unattended floor spills.

James Kauffman was wearing a jumpsuit and hadn't shaved in several days when he sat down on one side of a Plexiglas-shielded window and picked up a telephone. Carole, sitting on the other side of the glass, picked up the phone in front of her.

"He's not looking good in orange," she recalled, still upset by the memory of that first prison encounter and her reaction to all that had been happening. Simply put, she unloaded, detailing her anger, frustration, disappointment, embarrassment and shame.

"I'm sorry, I'm sorry, I'm sorry," James Kauffman kept repeating while his wife ticked off a litany of grievances and concerns.

She kept up the fire, telling him he'd been a jackass for waving a gun when the cops showed up at his door with the search warrant. Then she told him about the raid at her condo.

"I was flat-out angry that I was being put through this, but also scared of what was to follow," she said. He agreed that it had been stupid to wave a gun at the cops. But he insisted that he had had nothing to do with April's murder.

"He said he just couldn't handle the relentless pressure from the police regarding searches, and he lost control," she said.

A psychiatrist who examined James Kauffman subsequently explained to Carole that when people get "so humiliated, embarrassed and cornered," they can do something as irrational as brandishing a gun in the face of a police officer there to serve a warrant. It was kind of a martyr thing, the shrink said.

Still reeling from some of the things authorities told her as they went through the condo, Carole again asked her husband about the compound-cream scam. Once again he insisted that he hadn't done anything wrong.

"It's a very good cream, and I did prescribe it," he told her. "It's really effective" and "patients love it."

Once her anger subsided, Carole tried to focus on the issue at hand.

"How are we going to get you out of here?" she asked.

Eddie Jacobs was filing a motion for bail, Kauffman said. Others charged with more serious offenses, they both agreed, had gotten bail. Why shouldn't he? Maybe it would be house arrest. Maybe he'd have to wear an electronic ankle bracelet and report to authorities every day. At least he would be home and out of the hellhole that was the Atlantic County Jail.

But when the bail motion was heard, superior court judge Bernard DeLury accepted the arguments of the Atlantic County Prosecutor's Office and ruled that Kauffman was a flight risk and a danger to the community. Bail was denied. Jacobs would continue to fight the issue over the next several months through the appellate court system. Each motion was turned down. James Kauffman was to remain in jail.

Carole said her husband tried to make the best of the situation. Shortly after his arrest, his office was closed, and the state suspended his medical license. But behind bars he continued, in his way, to practice his profession. He ran into some corrections officers who were patients of his. So were some inmates. The doctor behind bars began to treat them and eventually was offering medical advice to inmates who had not been his patients. He told Carole the inmates were getting poor medical treatment from the prison and said he had urged them to demand better attention. He claimed that some prisoners were walking around the jail with broken bones that needed setting.

Some of the guards told him he shouldn't be dispensing medical advice. But he told Carole that his response to them was "I can't turn off who I am."

Just who James Kauffman was, of course, depended on who was being asked. To some he remained a dedicated physician who cared deeply about those who came to him for help. But to others he was a drug dealer dressed in hospital scrubs, a murderer hiding behind his medical practice.

Kauffman had been in jail about three months when he opened up about the depression that had been eating away at him since his arrest. Among other things, he told Carole that several of the guards were Pagans. (Andrew Glick said that was not true, but that there were some guards who rode bikes and a few who belonged to support clubs. In any event, the Pagans had eyes and ears inside the jail, a situation that added to James Kauffman's discomfort.)

In a letter dated September 1, 2017, Jimmy told Carole how he really felt and what he thought the future held. He predicted that he would never get out of jail alive.

"Dear Carole," he wrote. "I am beyond help. I feel bad in

every possible way. I am a political prisoner and I can't go on. They should have given me bail. I feel my life is effectively over. They will never let me out."

He then told Carole for the first time about the people he suspected of murdering April.

> *Approximately 5 or 6 months ago the garage door opened. I was accosted by two men with masks. They threw me to the concrete and put a gun to the back of my head + cocked it. They said they would come back + kill me if I talked. I assume they were in the motorcycle gang. I emailed Jacobs immediately and he decided I should not go to the police, which would open up a bigger can of worms. I didn't want to worry you but I got the guns for self-protection + unfortunately June 13th happened.*

Carole had her doubts about the story he was telling her. But she kept reading. He instructed her about what to do in the event of his death. He didn't want an obituary. He wanted to be buried in "the cheapest pine box" or cremated. "No shiva, or Kaddish"—the period of mourning and the traditional Jewish prayer—or any "graveside service," he insisted. But about a choice of burial, he wrote, "I would like to be next to you."

In the letter, he advised her to sell their time-shares in the Marriott Vacation Club and let his house in Linwood go into foreclosure. He told her to take the $600,000 in life insurance money that he was fighting for in the civil suit with Kim Pack. It was advice that Carole didn't take.

And he urged her to take back her maiden name.

"I am devastated this happened + they have won," he wrote, not specifying who "they" were. Jail, he wrote, was just too hard. "I can't take the captivity, food, noise + no sleep anymore along with not holding you."

Finally, he returned to the theme that was a constant in their rekindled romance: his lingering regrets over their youthful breakup.

> *I wish I was not that insecure young man so I could have had 40 not 4 happy years with you. You are the best + it is my loss.*
> *I apologize for the tear stains.*
> *I love you.*
>
> *Jim*

The letter underscored Carole's uncertainty. His explanations were beginning to sound forced, contrived, fake. There were just too many things that didn't make sense. Carole wanted to believe him. She wanted his story to be true. Maybe she wanted it too much. Maybe her desire to reconnect with her first love, with the boy she had dated in high school, had blinded her. Maybe she never really saw the man he had become.

TWELVE

Andrew Glick figured they would come early in the morning, just as they had when they arrested the doc. He could imagine how it would go down—a predawn raid conducted by a dozen cops and FBI agents, bulked up with flak jackets, armed with handguns and assault rifles as they fanned out around his property.

Instead, they came at night.

It was November 1, 2017, All Saints' Day on the Catholic calendar of his youth, a day off from school. Even before the raid, Glick said, it hadn't been a good day. His wife left that morning, packing her belongings in a car and heading out for Nebraska, where her sister lived. The marriage was over. She had filed for divorce. Glick wasn't going to fight it. In fact, he willingly gave her about $120,000 to help her "get started."

There were no children and no major assets, so the break would be clean.

The split had been coming for several months. The situation with the girlfriend and her children living in the home was untenable. Glick had moved her and her kids out back in September, finding an apartment in Ocean City. But the marriage was over by then.

"I got them an apartment after the summer rental season was over," he explained.

Glick also found himself a small efficiency unit at the corner of Eighth Street and the boardwalk that he began using as a stash house. It cost him $500 a month. He paid two months in advance. He had shut down his drug business in June after the raid on Kauffman's office, but by September he'd gone back into business. He moved his guns and drugs from the storage facility he was renting to the boardwalk apartment. It was easier access, and it drew less suspicion.

If the cops were watching him—and given the talk he had had with Scoppa, he figured they were—then having a small apartment a few blocks from where he had moved his girlfriend wouldn't arouse the kind of suspicion renting a storage facility would. Glick had four outbuildings on his property in Egg Harbor Township, so why would he need to rent a storage unit? That would have been a logical question investigators would ask. The efficiency apartment, on the other hand, might just have been a love nest.

He knew that he would have to vacate the efficiency in the spring, but at this point, he wasn't thinking that far ahead. He was in the moment, trying to assess what was going on and what he should do next. Among other things, his girlfriend told him that she might be pregnant.

"I'm thinking, how can I be a dad with all this going on?" Glick said.

It turned out to be a false alarm, one of the few positives to come out of the series of events that unfolded on November 1, 2017, Glick said later.

He worked a six a.m.–two p.m. shift that day and then, in a move he would soon regret, he swung by the apartment and collected his drugs and guns. He also swung by his girlfriend's apartment, where he had hidden drugs and cash in four different lamps. He brought everything back to the house.

"I guess I wanted to do an inventory, see what I had," he said.

He had rifles, including an AR-15 assault weapon, handguns and several hundred rounds of ammunition. He also had more than a pound of meth, several ounces of cocaine and cash totaling about $62,000.

That afternoon a regular customer swung by and bought two ounces of meth.

"He had originally called and said he wanted five," Glick said. "But when he got to my house, he said he only had enough money for two. I didn't think anything of it at the time, but after the raid, it made sense. The guy must have been working with the cops. If he asked for five and only took two, then they would be sure to find some drugs in the house when they conducted the raid."

As it would turn out, they found a lot more.

Glick was in the shed behind his house sorting out some things and stashing some of the drugs when he heard what sounded like a diesel-engine truck pulling up the long driveway that led from Ridge Avenue to his front door. It was around seven p.m. He had a flashlight in his hand as he stepped out of the shed to see what was going on.

Then he heard a voice.

"Andrew Glick, we have a search warrant."

His first thought was that one of his friends was busting his balls. Since the raid on the doc's office, everyone was talking about who would be next.

Not funny, he thought as he walked toward the gate that was part of a six-foot-high white privacy fence that surrounded his backyard. When he opened the gate, he saw a man pointing what looked like an AR-15 at his chest.

"Drop your weapon!" said the voice behind the gun.

Glick dropped his flashlight and was then ordered to lie facedown on the ground and put his hands behind his back. Zip tie handcuffs were quickly wrapped around his wrists. He was helped up and led to the front lawn, where he was again ordered to lie facedown. As he looked around from ground level, he saw an armada of police vehicles, and the ankles and boots of more than a dozen police officers scurrying across his property and heading for his front door.

Twenty minutes later he was brought inside and allowed to sit on a couch as the search intensified. They found all the drugs and guns and ammunition and a briefcase in which he had placed about $37,000. The drugs were stored in a blue Igloo ice chest he kept in the shed. So were most of the guns. But they missed another $25,000 he had hidden in a small gun case tucked under the cushions of the couch in the shed.

Within the hour Glick was hustled out of his home, placed in an SUV and driven to the FBI office in nearby Northfield. Glick's lawyer was called. Almost immediately there was talk about a cooperation agreement. This time Glick had few cards to play. He was told he was facing drug and weapons charges that could land him in jail for forty years. Did he want to help himself?

He jumped at the chance.

Glick spent about a week in the county jail before being released. Part of it was processing; part of it was working out the details of the cooperation agreement. And part of it was just to make the arrest look good. He was officially charged with two counts of possession and two counts of intent to distribute narcotics. On November 9, out on bail, Glick met with Fred Augello in the parking lot of a Wendy's in Northfield. Augello wanted to know what had happened. Glick told him he had been busted for drugs, but downplayed the case. He was going to fight the charges. He told Augello that his lawyer thought he had a chance to beat the rap. That, of course, was a lie, the first of many he would tell Freddy Augello over the next two months.

That meeting in the Wendy's parking lot would be followed by more than a dozen others in the following two months. At each he would record conversations for the Atlantic County Prosecutor's Office and the FBI.

"I was not happy doing this," he said, "but I had no choice."

Andrew Glick said he knew when he agreed to cooperate

that his life as an outlaw motorcycle gang member was over. But it wasn't until he began recording meetings with Augello that it really sank in.

"I was doing something that I had preached against my whole life," he said. "It went against everything I believed in, everything being in a club was all about. It was something I never thought I would ever do and every time I had to do it, I said to myself, 'This sucks.'"

But he did it.

It was a matter of survival. He thought he was looking at forty years in prison for the drug and weapons charges. He didn't want to spend what could amount to the rest of his life in a state prison. So he agreed to cooperate, tell authorities what he knew about the murder, and record conversations. They, in turn, agreed to lower the charges to drug possession and distribution and to tell his judge about his cooperation at the time of sentencing. That was the trade-off. Andrew Glick said he didn't want to go to jail, so he gave up a piece of himself and agreed to cooperate.

In fact, he would end up with an even better deal. All of the charges against him were dropped.

"I've lost my name and my credibility," Glick said as he sat in a diner in South Jersey more than a year after he had wired up and several months after he had taken the witness stand in the case against Augello. "I was one of the most respected guys in the club. I was proud to be a Pagan. I lost the respect and honor everybody gave me. I was . . . a good leader. I'm never gonna have that. I'll never be in another club. I'll be a guy who rides by himself.

"I'm just a guy who turned. Just another dumb ass who co-operated."

Still, even at that late date, Glick made a distinction between what he had done and what Pagan cooperators had brought to the table in other cases.

"I only gave up Fred," he said. "It was never about the Pagans. In fact, the whole pill mill operation wasn't a Pagans thing. It was Freddy Augello's thing. Freddy's crime world. Look, I did what I had to do. Is it something I'm proud of? No. But if you're looking at forty years in jail, you don't have that many choices. I did what I did, and I have to live with it."

Glick's testimony and the recordings he made would become the building blocks on which the case against Fred Augello was mounted. Tapes can be devastating pieces of evidence. Defense attorneys can attack the credibility and testimony of witnesses like Andrew Glick. They can raise questions about his motivation ("You're just doing this to get out from under your own criminal problems, to avoid a forty-year prison sentence") and point to his own criminal history and background ("How long have you been a drug dealer?").

But what a defense attorney can't do is challenge his client's own words from a secretly recorded conversation played in front of a jury. Major organized crime and narco trafficking cases in courts all over the country have included tapes of wise-guys and drug dealers discussing all manner of murder and mayhem. "You gotta get them when they don't expect no problem," a Philadelphia mob boss once said while outlining his plan to lure rivals to a meeting and then shoot them in the head. "Over here. Over here is best, behind the ear." And a South

Jersey heroin dealer put the final nail in his own coffin when he told an associate (who was wearing a body wire) why he couldn't stop dealing. "It's the most money I can make," he said as the tape picked up every word. "I like to spend money."

The Augello tapes weren't as dramatic. There is not one tape on which Augello overtly incriminates himself. Instead, there are rambling conversations in which he and Glick talk around the specifics of the April Kauffman murder. Other tapes, however, provide clear references to Augello's desire to have James Kauffman killed in prison. Augello, the tapes indicate, was clearly worried about Kauffman cooperating and about what he might have been telling authorities. On one tape, he confronted Glick, asking him straight out if he was wearing a wire. Glick denied it, and Augello later apologized, but the confrontation underscored Augello's paranoia.

Glick wore two "bugs" each time they met. One was designed to look like a credit card, the other like a ballpoint pen. Both were in the front pocket of whatever shirt he was wearing. Sometimes he also had a small camera that looked like a button. But Augello was fidgety and constantly moving around. It was difficult, Glick said, to keep him on camera. The easiest time to get a video recording was when they met in a restaurant and Augello was stationary, sitting across the table from him. But that rarely happened. Most times they met in the parking lots of local restaurants, sitting in the cabin of Augello's van. The other problem with the camera button, Glick said, was that it required a wire that was strapped to Glick's chest. If Freddy ever patted him down, the undercover operation would blow up.

"They told me if he patted me down and found the wire that the jig would be up, to do what I had to do to get out of there and they would back me up," Glick said. "We didn't use the camera all the time because of the problems that it could create."

All of the meetings occurred with law enforcement surveillance teams—FBI agents or detectives from the Atlantic County Prosecutor's Office—nearby. Anytime Glick got a call from Augello, detectives were listening in.

"They had given me a new cell phone, and anytime it rang, the call also rang on a phone they had so they could hear what was being said," Glick explained. "Whenever Freddy called and asked for a meeting, they knew about it right away. Sometimes I'd have to stall and make excuses. If he wanted to meet in ten minutes, I'd say I had to do something first, walk my dogs or do something in the yard. This would give me time to swing by the office and get the listening devices and allowed them to set up surveillance."

Paranoid and concerned about wiretaps and room bugs—justifiably, it would turn out—Augello would never say anything of significance on the phone, and even in the conversations in his van and at his home, he was circumspect. Sometimes he would turn up the volume on the radio. Other times he would take out a sheet of paper and write something on it, show it to Glick and then fold the paper up and put it in his pocket. He also insisted that Glick leave his own cell phone in his own truck, convinced that authorities had the technological ability to tap into conversations through a linkup with someone's phone.

"By that point he was pretty paranoid," Glick said. "He knew I had been arrested, and I guess he wondered about me. And he knew his name was popping up more and more in the murder investigation."

Still, he missed some obvious signs.

One of the early meetings was scheduled for a restaurant, the Cheese Board, on New Road in Linwood. By the time Glick and then Augello arrived, the FBI had already set up surveillance at two tables. One agent was sitting alone, Glick said. Another was with a woman. Both tables provided clear views of the table where Augello and Glick were seated. Augello told Glick he wanted some breakfast, an omelet. But it was eleven thirty, and the restaurant had stopped serving breakfast.

"He insisted he wanted an omelet, not lunch," Glick said, "so we went across the street to another restaurant, Romanelli's. They were still serving breakfast."

Glick was wired for sound, of course. And Augello was circumspect as always in what he said. But what he didn't notice was that as he ate and talked, both the couple and the man who had been sitting alone at the Cheese Board made their way into Romanelli's, took seats at different tables, placed their orders and watched as he and Glick discussed business.

Some of the conversations went on for more than an hour. Many were disjointed. In several Augello denied having had anything to do with the murder of April Kauffman. Glick, who over the years had had several conversations in which Augello told him just the opposite, figured this was all part of Freddy's defense in the event there was a listening device nearby.

Augello called the prosecution's theory of the case a "fantasy" and said investigators were looking for a "scapegoat."

"Unless I'm . . . incorrect here I don't . . . think you murdered this guy's wife. Did you?" Augello said in one of the first conversations recorded by Glick. Then he added, "I didn't murder this guy's wife so . . . so who are these . . . where is this murderer? You know what I mean?"

The comment set the tone for virtually every conversation that followed. Augello denied knowing Jim Kauffman and Francis Mulholland and insisted again and again that he had had nothing to do with April Kauffman's murder.

But one thing that clearly piqued his interest, Glick said, was a report that Kauffman might have been cooperating and that the doctor had already given up details about the murder in the hopes of working out a deal for himself. There were two letters Kauffman's lawyer, Edwin Jacobs Jr., had sent to authorities during the investigation—letters that pointed to possible suspects in the murder of April Kauffman. One of the letters specifically mentioned the names of Freddy Augello and Francis Mulholland as individuals who might have been involved.

Glick told Augello he had learned about this from his own defense attorney and claimed he could get a copy of that letter because it might figure in his pending drug case. It was a plausible explanation and enabled authorities to use the letter to push Augello's buttons.

The biker bit.

"Well, that's bizarre," Augello said of the information implicating him and Francis Mulholland. "I . . . I don't know why this guy [Kauffman] would say that about me."

"And . . . and who is Francis?" he asked before returning to the issue of how Kauffman had come up with the names. "Where did he get my name from? . . . Just out of the blue?"

Augello pressed Glick, telling him it was important that he see the letter that Kauffman's lawyer had sent to the prosecutor's office. The investigators monitoring the recorded conversations were only too happy to comply. Their goal was to get Augello talking in the hopes that he would incriminate himself in the murder.

"Freddy's concern was that the doc would cut a deal with the feds who were after him in the compound-cream case," Glick said. "He said the doc knew he was never going to beat that and that he was looking at life in the murder case. Freddy figured the doc would work out a deal that would make life in prison a little easier, you know, a cell in some federal prison where he could live out his days. . . . Freddy was afraid the doc was going to give us all up."

These were things that Glick said were referred to obliquely during the conversations, often in written notes that Augello showed him and then pocketed. One of the first notes that Augello wrote, Glick said, was about a plan to keep Jim Kauffman, then an inmate in the Atlantic County Jail, from talking.

"Well, here's the deal, dude," Augello said. "I'll get rid of this. I'll write it here. Don't say it."

The tape picks up what sounds like the scratching of someone writing on a piece of paper.

"Can you read that?" Augello asks.

"Um-huh," says Glick.

"That's what's gonna happen," Augello says as the tape

picks up what sounds like a piece of paper being ripped from a notepad.

"That, that would be a game changer," says Glick.

"I have some friends in Philly," Glick said Augello wrote as they sat in his van in the parking lot of a Wendy's. "They're going to get the doc in jail."

That note, Glick would later testify, was when Augello first proposed having James Kauffman killed in prison. He was telling Glick that he would use his organized crime connections to have the hit carried out.

Augello's "friends in Philly" was a reference to his reputed ties to members of the Philadelphia mob. During this part of the investigation authorities who had Augello under constant surveillance would videotape a meeting he had in the Borgata casino-hotel in Atlantic City with a reputed mob associate. But Augello would later tell Glick that the Philly guys weren't interested.

For authorities tracking the case, that would have been the second time mobsters turned Augello down. The first, investigative sources have said, had been when he was seeking someone to carry out the contract on April Kauffman. In both instances, Augello's offer was one the mob decided it could refuse.

After Augello's attempt to recruit mobsters failed, Glick claimed that his Mexican drug cartel suppliers were willing to have Kauffman killed. Augello was pleased with that plan and encouraged Glick to follow through with it. All of that, of course, was a fiction. But the conversations reinforced the murder conspiracy charge that would eventually be lodged against Augello for plotting to have the doctor murdered.

In the taped conversations, Augello also explained why he

was writing notes and why he was reluctant to say anything over the phone.

"I'm convinced that my phone is tapped. That's why I told you I've done nothing wrong, and the only thing you've done wrong is you got caught [with drugs]. . . . So that's where we are at. That's why I talk to you about this like this and . . . and I am totally convinced that they are, that every time I talk to you on the phone, they are listening."

Augello acknowledged that some members of the club were involved in a pill mill with Kauffman, but said that had nothing to do with him. He dismissed questions Glick said authorities were asking about Stevie Wittenwiler and Glenn Seeler. Augello described each one of them as a "loser." Wittenwiler, who had been the original contact in the pill mill scam, had been kicked out of the club. Seeler had moved with his wife to North Carolina. Augello said it didn't matter to him what any of them had been doing with Kauffman.

"So you got a couple guys that are banged up from riding motorcycles. They are getting pills they like to eat. That doesn't mean they murdered his wife," he said as Glick's recording device picked up his every word. "You know what I mean?"

Later he added, "Let's say all these people were getting drugs from this guy . . . and some of the people were selling them. . . . What does that have to do with a dead person, is what I'm getting at. . . . Sounds like a bunch of fucking bullshit."

Augello was also concerned about the pressure that seemed to be building in the April Kauffman murder case.

"How come they didn't do this fucking five years ago?" he wondered.

Both he and Glick speculated that political pressure had been put on the prosecutor's office back in 2012 and 2013 to scuttle the investigation because, they both agreed, there were people in high office who were concerned that the names of some influential people who were sleeping with April would have been made public.

When Damon Tyner was appointed prosecutor in 2017, he set out to review all cold cases and made the April Kauffman murder a top priority. Glick, armed with information provided by investigators, told Augello that it looked like Kauffman had been giving information to investigators as far back as 2012. That, he said, was when Kauffman's lawyer sent a letter to the prosecutor's office suggesting possible scenarios for the murder. These apparently included some of the same scenarios Kauffman had laid out in his deposition in the life insurance civil suit. None of it had been made public at the time, but the information allowed Glick to get Augello talking about the murder. Possible suspects, the doctor had said at that deposition, might include a mentally troubled military veteran with whom April had come in contact, angry members of the Linwood police department with whom she was constantly clashing and members of an outlaw biker gang she had met while riding.

A copy of the second, follow-up letter written by Jacobs and sent to the prosecutor's office in March 2017 expanded on the biker angle. This was the letter Augello wanted to see.

Addressed to Erik M. Bergman, then the chief assistant prosecutor, the letter read in part: "This letter is a supplement to my October 4, 2012 correspondence. . . . [T]he names Francis Mulholland and Ferdinand C. Augello have been brought to my attention. As to the latter, he may be a resident of Absecon or Ocean View, New Jersey. Either or both may have an association with the Pagan Motorcycle Club. We know nothing of the accuracy or reliability of this information."

"The guy was trying to throw me under the bus," Augello said of Jim Kauffman after Glick had shown him the letter.

"From the beginning," Glick added.

Augello said repeatedly that prescribing oxycodone as Kauffman had done was "unethical" even though it might not have been illegal. But that was on the doctor and those who went to him as patients. Augello pointed out on several of the tapes that he was never a patient and said, "I'm not going to jail for murdering some woman I didn't murder."

Those were the continuing themes whenever the April Kauffman–pill mill murder case was discussed. Augello was consistent in his verbal denials, although Glick said the notes he was writing told a different story.

In order to add more pressure, Glick told Augello that after he was released on bail in the drug case, investigators sarcastically told him to "have a good Thanksgiving," implying that it might be his last as a free man. They also said they intended to "solve" the April Kauffman murder "by the end of the year."

"They're just gonna . . . just make a . . . round everybody fuckin' up, charge them all with conspiracy fuckin' for murder and see fuckin' who talks," Glick said in explaining what he perceived as the prosecutor's strategy. In fact, that was pretty close to reality.

Augello continued to insist that he was innocent, that investigators were looking for a "scapegoat" and that Kauffman's actions didn't make any sense.

"Let's say, hypothetically, Kauffman paid somebody to whack his wife," Augello said on one tape. "Anybody, right? . . . So why would he . . . why would he point the finger at anybody else if he was involved? . . . The whole thing's retarded."

It was a logical question to ask. And the implications were clear to both Augello and Glick. By pointing a finger at Augello, Kauffman was trying to get out from under his own criminal liability. Either he was going to claim that he too was the victim of a Pagans' extortion-murder plot, or he was going to try to cut a deal for himself that would land him in some country club–like federal prison for the rest of his life.

But none of it really mattered, Augello said, because "we haven't done anything wrong."

It was all, he said, a "fucking fantasy."

Andrew Glick recorded his last conversation for authorities on January 5, 2018. Three days later he met with John Kachbalian at Kachbalian's home. The Egyptian asked about the drug case against Glick and told Glick to stay strong, that he could do the time in prison and that he would be back on his bike when he got out.

"Be righteous," he said the Egyptian told him.

They also talked about what was going on in the biker underworld: the internal bickering and petty backbiting that had led Glick to step away from the club. All of that could be straightened out, said Kachbalian, who had had his own problems with some Pagan leaders. It was a casual, rambling conversation, just two friends who shared common interests and who believed in the "life."

"I told him I appreciated everything he had done for me," Glick said in recounting that last meeting with Kachbalian. "I said I respected him and wanted to thank him."

Only Glick knew that their meeting that day would be their last. In his way, he tried to tell Kachbalian as much.

Both men had been fans of a History Channel series called *Gangland Undercover.* The series ran for two seasons and was based on the real-life undercover work of a federal informant who had infiltrated two different biker gangs. The informant, Charles Falco, worked for the Bureau of Alcohol, Tobacco, Firearms and Explosives. Falco had gone undercover to build cases against the Mongols and the Vagos, California-based biker gangs. During one of his undercover stints, Falco posed as a biker whose nickname was "Chef."

Kachbalian and Glick would always joke about that.

As he was leaving Kachbalian on the afternoon of January 8, 2018, Glick made a passing reference to the show and told the Egyptian, "It's weird how stuff plays out, how things eventually become true. Falco was Chef, and now Chef is Falco. I just want you to know I'll never forget you, brother."

Kachbalian looked puzzled, Glick said, and tried to ask him what he meant, but Glick, who was sitting behind the wheel of his pickup truck at the time, never looked back. He just drove away.

On January 9, 2018, Atlantic County prosecutor Damon Tyner announced that arrests had been made in connection with the murder of April Kauffman. Those charged included

Fred Augello, Joseph "Irish" Mulholland and Dr. James Kauffman, who was already in custody. Several other individuals tied to a pill mill operation run by the Pagans and James Kauffman had been arrested on drug trafficking charges, the prosecutor said. And Augello had also been charged with conspiracy to kill James Kauffman.

The *Press of Atlantic City* called the press conference in which the arrests were announced "brief but explosive" and said the announcement had ended "years of speculation." Tyner told reporters, "For the past 5½ years since April Kauffman was found shot to death inside her home in Linwood, New Jersey, there has been little movement in the case and no arrests have been made in connection with the murder. That is, until today."

The prosecutor said James Kauffman wanted his wife dead because she was threatening to expose the pill mill ring and because she wanted a divorce. James Kauffman, Tyner said, chose to "have her killed as opposed to losing his financial empire, as he described it to several individuals."

The mention of "individuals" was the first hint that authorities had information provided by cooperating witnesses.

That day Glick had a message on his phone. It was from Kachbalian. He was warning him that authorities were staging raids and arresting people in connection with the pill mill and the murder.

"They're rounding everybody up," Kachbalian said on the message. "Call me if you have the chance."

THIRTEEN

Carole Weintraub watched Tyner's press conference on the Internet. She couldn't believe what she was hearing. How had this all happened? And how did she fit into the picture? She saw herself cast as the new wife of the sleazy, drug-dealing doctor who had killed the woman who had shared her husband's bed before her. *This isn't happening,* she thought. She had spent her entire life trying to build a good reputation. And now, "I just felt it had all gone up in smoke."

She was ashamed and mortified, she said. "I remember googling my name, and all of this nonsense would come in."

And it would get worse.

Ten days after the arrests were announced, James Kauffman was scheduled to appear in Atlantic County Superior Court to enter a plea to charges of murder, conspiracy and drug dealing.

In the courtroom, Carole was shocked by her husband's appearance. He was dressed in an orange prison jumpsuit and looked worn and haggard. His hair, which he used to dye, had turned white. He looked around the room. Their eyes met.

"It was one of the most devastating things I had ever seen," she said. "Here's this man who I had known as a kid and later as an adult who came out in a jumpsuit, handcuffs and leg irons.

"I just thought, who is this? Why is he here? What has he done? I thought I was just dealing with somebody who was sloppy with guns."

The thought that there might have been more frightened her. She felt angry, confused, betrayed. But she was still in her husband's corner. She still wanted to believe in his innocence.

"There was a part of me that felt sorry for him," she said. "It's part of my nature. . . . There was another part of me that felt like . . . what's going on here? Please, please, somebody tell me what's the truth. I can't live with this ambiguity."

She watched as the prosecutor outlined a pyramid that he described as an illegal drug ring run by the Pagans. At the top of the pyramid was James Kauffman, the doctor who had written the prescriptions.

Carole, who had a lifetime of playing by the rules, had no references to draw on for the situation that her husband was now in. She thought about the worst thing she had ever gotten in trouble for in her entire life. She had to go all the way back to junior high, in Mrs. Sheehan's social studies class, when she got caught giving somebody the answers to a quiz. And here was her husband facing drug-dealing and murder charges. It was all too much.

The prisoner pleaded not guilty. When it came time to argue bail, Judge DeLury again denied the motion. The judge explained that if he let him out, James Kauffman would be "very likely to be involved in obstruction and intimidation of witnesses."

"I was devastated," Carole said. "I didn't know where to put myself. I didn't know what to do," she said. After her husband pleaded not guilty, "I got up, put my lipstick on and went out the door."

Family members and friends of the other defendants in the case were dealing with the same kind of emotional turmoil. Augello, Joseph Mulholland, Paul Pagano and Tabitha Chapman, the thirty-five-year-old daughter of a woman whom Augello was dating, were picked up in Atlantic County. Authorities went south to arrest Glenn Seeler, Cheryl Pizza and Beverly Augello.

Over the next few months, most of them would, through their lawyers, negotiate deals with the government and agree to testify. Only Pagano, a veteran biker and longtime Pagan, would "be righteous."

Sitting in a police station in Summerland Key around six a.m. on January 9, Beverly Augello was told by investigators that she had a serious problem and that now was the time to help herself.

At first she claimed that Kauffman was just her doctor.

"I don't know anything about this," she said when two Atlantic County detectives who were sent to pick her up told her about the pill mill and murder investigation.

"You have to worry about yourself," one of the detectives

told her. "It's important for you to understand. Don't dig yourself a bigger hole."

She said she was just "trying to leave New Jersey in the past."
Then she began to cry. The investigators offered to get her a
cup of coffee and a cigarette. They continued to urge her to
look out for herself.

"We have good information, very good evidence," she was
told. "You have to think about how you want to do this."

That morning she began to give up part of the story, admitting that she had picked up an envelope during one of her visits
to James Kauffman's office. She hedged, however, when asked
who had given her the envelope and whom she, in turn, gave it
to. She wasn't sure exactly when this had happened, she said.
But she was sure it was sometime after the Super Bowl in which
Nicki Minaj had performed. (Minaj performed in Super Bowl
XLVI in February 2012.) She also said she had had no idea
what was inside the envelope and that she had never looked.

Eventually she would provide more specific details. And she
would testify that at the request of her ex-husband she had
picked up that envelope from James Kauffman on the morning
April Kauffman was killed. She said she brought the envelope
to Fred Augello, but never looked inside.

Joseph "Irish" Mulholland, who was facing both murder and
drug charges, also was quick to work out a deal. Interviewed by
Detective Scoppa and FBI agent Daniel Garrabrant shortly after his arrest on January 9, Mulholland was told that there was
"sufficient evidence" to convict him.

But the investigators also told him they knew that he had
been in a drug rehabilitation program, that he was trying to

turn his life around and that if he had been "roped into some dumb stuff," now was the time to make things right.

"You're not the same guy you used to be," Garrabrant said. "You were a fucking mess back then."

During that first session, Mulholland admitted that he had introduced Francis Mulholland to Fred Augello, but that was as far as he was willing to go.

The arrests were highlighted in newspaper and television reports and became the talk of social media. Bloggers in Atlantic County began posting about the daily developments in the case. And on Facebook anyone and everyone weighed in. This included John Kachbalian. The Egyptian understood how the system worked. After the arrests were made public and Andrew Glick had not been charged, he knew the Chef had gone bad. His Facebook posts began to trumpet that fact.

One in particular struck Andrew Glick as both clever and on point.

"Ridge Avenue Pharmacy Closed Due to Rat Infestation" read the post that Glick thought was funny even though his law enforcement handlers didn't.

"I had taken off on January ninth," Glick said. "Scoppa told me to get out of town for a while."

He spent about a week on the road with stops in Maryland, Virginia and Delaware. But then he came back.

"I couldn't stand it," he said of his brief stint away from home. "I borrowed an AR-15 from a friend. He had made some adjustments, and it was fully automatic. He also gave me some ammunition. I went back to my house on Ridge Avenue."

Glick would stay there for the next eighteen months, through the trial, his stint on the witness stand and the sentencing of Freddy Augello. He was cautious, careful about where he went and whom he associated with, but he wasn't going to live in hiding. The Egg Harbor Township Police would routinely drive by the house and stop in if anything looked suspicious.

One afternoon Glick called up a hooker he knew and asked her to make a house call. Her driver stayed outside in the car.

"I'm just about to get it on," he said with a laugh, "when I hear this knock on the door. It's the cops, and they got the driver in handcuffs. They asked me if I knew him and if everything was all right."

Glick told the police that he had a woman in doing some housecleaning and the guy was her driver. He said the guy didn't want to wait in the house while she worked, so he stayed outside in the car. No problem.

It was the law enforcement version of coitus interruptus. But the hooker was very impressed.

"The police around here are really vigilant," she said, assuming the cops had made a routine stop after seeing a different car than usual in the driveway.

"They're very good," Glick agreed, deciding it was better if she had no idea he was being watched.

That he was a cooperator in the case was quickly becoming common knowledge. Whether anyone would try to do anything about it was another matter. He just decided that he would be ready and that whatever happened, happened. His philosophy, as an outlaw biker and now as a cooperating witness, never changed: plan for the worst, hope for the best.

Not everyone involved in the case was capable of adopting that approach. James Kauffman, in particular, was having serious problems coping. Shortly after the murder charge was announced, he was transferred to the Hudson County Jail in Kearny, New Jersey. This, in theory, was a security move. Fred Augello was now an inmate in Atlantic County, and given the threats he had made in his conversations with Glick, authorities thought it wise to relocate the doctor.

Why the Hudson County Jail was chosen has never been made clear. Located 120 miles north of Atlantic City, the correctional facility is home to about 1,200 inmates, many of them drug dealers and gangbangers from the northern part of the state. There are at least ten county jails closer to Atlantic County. Any one of those, it would turn out, might have been a better location.

"He was ostensibly moved for his own protection," said Carole Weintraub, who was concerned about the threats but realized there wasn't much she could do about them.

"My feeling was that if somebody wants to get you, they'll get you," she said. In jail, it's a "chip shot." All they have to do is "get past a CO who's making forty thousand dollars."

But of all the county jails in New Jersey, she wondered—and continues to wonder—why was Hudson County chosen? It was, she said, the "most horrible environment that they could think of." Maybe authorities were trying to punish her husband even before he had been convicted. Between June 2017 and March 2018, six inmates died at the Hudson County Jail; four of the deaths were classified as suicides.

"That remains a mystery," Edwin Jacobs said when asked

why his client was transferred to Hudson County. "I've never been given an explanation. . . . I can't understand the move so far away."

Jacobs said he believed his client should have been granted bail, which would have made questions about the Hudson County transfer and what happened there moot. But the fact that he was denied bail and then shipped to a county jail hours away added to James Kauffman's deteriorating mental state and growing depression.

James Kauffman's stay in the Hudson County facility ended in less than three weeks.

At nine thirty a.m. on January 26, 2018, Carole got a call from a jail chaplain.

"I'm sorry to inform you," he said. Then his words started to run together. What Carole knew was that Jimmy was dead. "He committed suicide," the chaplain said.

Carole was in shock. She picked up the phone and called Jacobs. He advised her to leave her apartment to avoid the media. So Carole hid out at a friend's house, where she used her cell phone to make a flurry of calls. But she couldn't get any more information.

"The Hudson County Jail was extremely uncooperative," she said. "They stonewalled me at every turn."

Meanwhile, the hometown newspaper was doing better at gathering information about the latest twist in the April Kauffman murder case. The *Press of Atlantic City* reported that Dr. James Kauffman was found dead at nine twenty a.m. The newspaper quoted sources as saying the suicide was "carefully planned," and that Kauffman was found "face-down in the cell with a torn piece of bed sheet [sic] twisted into a wire-tight rope that was looped around his neck and around the bunk.

"A long suicide note also was left near his bed, sources said."

The newspaper reported that Kauffman was not on suicide watch, but was being held in maximum security because of the murder charge against him.

"I feel bad for his widow," Jacobs told the newspaper. "I think all the things that occurred in the last five years took a toll on Jim."

Jacobs, in an interview at his Atlantic City office months later, would expand on that theory.

"Him being pretrial detained was off-the-charts wrong," said the criminal defense attorney while pointing out that he has had clients, including organized crime figures charged with serious crimes, who have been granted bail. And the transfer to Hudson County was "inexplicable." All of that contributed to "an obvious deterioration of his physical and mental" condition that began with a "pretrial detention that should have never happened."

Others, however, said James Kauffman realized he had no way out and decided to leave on his own terms.

"I think that Dr. Kauffman realized he'd been found out," Patrick D'Arcy, Kim Pack's lawyer, told the newspaper. "The jig was up."

Carole said she knew her husband was depressed, but never thought he would take his own life. She said that two psychiatrists had examined her husband in jail, one hired by his defense lawyer and another who worked for the prison, and they both came to the same conclusion: James Kauffman wasn't a suicide risk.

"I couldn't make sense of it," Carole said. "Why would he do that? I don't get it." But, she added, "He could be mercurial."

Carole wanted to hold a memorial service at Rodeph Shalom, where only four years earlier, she and Jimmy had been married. But her friends convinced her not to because her synagogue could not protect her from the media. Instead, she held a memorial service at the Symphony House, where her condo was located and where the staff was able to keep unwanted visitors from attending.

More than fifty people showed up. Five congregants, including Carole, lit five candles in Jim Kauffman's memory. Carole's rabbi spoke about the sanctity of life. The mourners read scripture and recited traditional memorial prayers.

At the end, Carole stood up and tearfully thanked everyone for being there, especially her daughter, Abby, whom she knew wasn't fond of her husband.

"With very few exceptions, every life has value," Carole said of her decision to hold a memorial. "There was good in him. I wanted to honor the good in Jimmy's life."

Honoring her husband's request, Carole had arranged to have Jimmy's remains cremated. An undertaker traveled to Hudson County and handled all the details. Carole never saw the body. And, despite her repeated requests, she was not given the suicide note.

Because of the pending murder case in which Fred Augello was now the chief defendant, Judge DeLury ruled the suicide note was evidence. He placed it under seal and ruled that neither Carole nor Edwin Jacobs Jr. could see it.

In the months after the death, Carole struggled to understand what had happened and, more important, why it had happened. She was left with an urn filled with ashes and a series of questions without satisfactory answers: a set of facts covered in ambiguity.

Her friends in Atlantic City told her there were rumors all over the island. Jimmy had been murdered in jail. He was killed by the Pagans. No, he was killed by the politicians and people in high places who had slept with April and wanted to keep it quiet. He was still alive. He had faked his death with the help of the authorities and was now in protective custody. He would be a surprise witness at the murder trial and in the multimillion-dollar compound-cream case and would be whisked away into the Witness Protection Program.

Andrew Glick, for a time at least, thought that the "suicide" had been staged. It was part of that "umbrella" that had been placed over Kauffman from the beginning, he said. The murder case had finally been broken, but without Kauffman at the defense table, there would be no reason to delve into his troubled marriage and the relationships April might have had with others.

While Carole Weintraub continued to cling to the belief—or hope—that her husband was somehow a victim, Glick saw the doc as a malevolent manipulator who was capable of orchestrating events from behind bars in some witness-security wing of a federal prison. For a time he toyed with the idea that the doc was still alive, but he eventually came around to the belief that James Kauffman had died a coward's death. Unable to deal with the consequences of his own actions, the doc had taken his own life.

That death, just like the death of April Kauffman, left many unanswered questions.

To this day, Glick believes that James Kauffman, not Francis Mulholland, pumped the two bullets that killed her into April Kauffman.

"Mulholland was just a patsy, a scapegoat. That's what I think," Glick said on more than one occasion as he sat in a South Jersey diner, recounting the story in the months before and after the trial. "The doc only had once chance, and he wasn't going to depend on a junkie."

Glick's theory is that April Kauffman was already dead when Francis Mulholland walked into her bedroom that morning. Mulholland fired two shots, one into the bed and the other into the wall. That would account for the four bullets mentioned in the police report. It would also explain the text message sent to Billy Gonzalez around three thirty on the morning of the shooting, the text message in which April said she would see him in the morning. She had said virtually the same thing when Gonzalez had dropped her off at her home on the afternoon of May 9. There was no need for the text message. It wasn't April who sent that message, Glick believes, but rather James Kauffman, who was attempting to bolster the story he would tell police: the story that his wife was still alive when he left the house for work shortly after five a.m. on May 10, 2012. Glick's theory also would fit with the one autopsy report that put April Kauffman's time of death at around two a.m. At least two other reports placed the time of death at around five thirty a.m., which fit better with the theory adopted by investigators.

None of that, of course, changed the principal facts of the

case. James Kauffman wanted his wife dead and paid Freddy Augello to set up the hit. The conspiracy to murder April Kauffman was part of whichever theory was being presented, and a conviction based on either theory was still valid.

Who really pulled the trigger is almost immaterial. But if, as Glick believes, it was James Kauffman, then the "overdose" death of Frank Mulholland eliminated the only person who could have pointed a finger directly at the doctor. Fred Augello and Joseph Mulholland played the same roles in the conspiracy regardless of who had fired the fatal shots. James Kauffman's death sealed the deal. No one would ever know exactly what happened that morning.

Alone at home, Carole Weintraub wondered what to believe. For a time she even questioned whose ashes were in that urn the undertaker had given her and that she kept in a spare bedroom, behind a TV set.

But she had little time for introspection. The publicity surrounding the murder, the suicide and the pending trial of Freddy Augello brought her unwanted and, she would argue, unwarranted attention.

She declined every interview request, but the media spotlight continued to focus on her.

On April 9, 2018, Phillyvoice.com, a news website in Philadelphia, ran a story by reporter Kevin C. Shelly under the headline "Prosecutors move to seize Kauffman's $1M luxury condo in Philly."

In his report, Shelly wrote that James and Carole Kauffman

co-owned a luxury condo in the Symphony House, a condo for which "they paid $982,000 . . . according to tax records." Carole said the condo had actually cost $1.35 million. She said the $982,000 was an apparent reference to a condo in the Old City section of Philadelphia that she had purchased earlier and then sold when she moved to the Symphony House. She had put her husband's name on both properties, but had made the purchases with her own money. Placing Jimmy's name on the deeds was a move that she had come to regret, but one that she had to deal with in the aftermath of the arrest and suicide of her husband.

The story disclosed that in their motion, prosecutors were also attempting to seize the seven-thousand-square-foot house in Linwood, New Jersey, where April Kauffman had been murdered. James Kauffman became the property's sole owner after her death.

"Kauffman's last wife, Carole L. Weintraub, whom he married a year after April Kauffman's murder, appears to never have been added to the Linwood deed," the story noted. In fact, Carole Weintraub never wanted anything to do with that particular piece of real estate and never spent any time there.

The story then went on to rehash the suicide, noting that "According to authorities, the disgraced endocrinologist strangled himself with a bedsheet on Jan. 26 while alone in his jail cell."

And it concluded by disclosing that during the raids that were carried out in June 2017 police had seized $68,407 in cash from the condo, $29,390 from the Linwood home, $10,000 from Kauffman's medical office in Egg Harbor Township, and $687 from his SUV. The police also confiscated a profit-sharing plan valued for $128,901, an IRA valued at $40,000, a car and a Harley-Davidson motorcycle.

Carole said that the police did not confiscate the profit-sharing plan or the IRA and that she ultimately used the cash in the IRA to pay her husband's lawyer. While the details in the news report may not have been completely accurate, the story in total was a retelling of the nightmare she had been living for months.

She wondered if it would ever end.

FOURTEEN

Andrew Glick decided that he wasn't going to let John Kachbalian or anyone else set the agenda in the run-up to the Freddy Augello trial. The Egyptian had continued to post on Facebook about the case, first implying and then declaring that Glick was cooperating even though there had been no formal announcement from the prosecutor's office.

Eventually a witness list would surface and remove all doubt, but shortly after the arrests, Glick decided to make a preemptive move. Much to the chagrin of Scoppa and other investigators working the case, Glick reached out to Peter Edwards, a reporter at the *Toronto Star* who had written extensively about the biker underworld and the violent motorcycle gang wars in Canada.

On March 8, 2018, a story based on Edwards's telephone

interview with Glick appeared in the paper. Looking for a local angle, Edwards asked Glick about reports that the Pagans had considered expanding into Canada. Glick said that was true, but that the club had decided not to make that move because of a potential clash with the Canadian branch of the Hells Angels and because of tough Canadian laws aimed at criminal gang activity. The article described Glick as "a longtime American bike gang leader who's now a key prosecution witness in an upcoming murder-for-hire trial in New Jersey that's centered around the illegal opioid trade."

The article went on to describe the violent biker underworld and the Pagans' role in it, noting that one of the club's mottos was "There's nothing a pickaxe can't solve."

The second half of the story focused on the April Kauffman murder investigation and the pill mill operation. Edwards wrote that Glick was "always against" killing April Kauffman but said that James Kauffman constantly pushed for the murder.

"The doc kept complaining, 'Why is it taking so long?'" Glick is quoted as saying in the newspaper story. "I said, 'We're working on it. It's not like there's a store where we can go to hire hitmen to kill women.'"

The article ended with Glick saying he was concerned for his safety and would be constantly looking over his shoulder.

That kind of pretrial publicity is not something that prosecutors are happy about. Detective Scoppa was upset, but Glick said he told him he didn't want Kachbalian or anyone else— bloggers and Facebook commentators were all over the story— setting the agenda.

"I just decided to out myself," Glick said matter-of-factly

while explaining his thinking as he munched on a cheesesteak sandwich in a local diner a few months after the story broke.

Eventually a witness list, which included the names of Glick and the defendants who had decided to cooperate, would pop up on social media. Kachbalian was ultimately cited criminally for some of his posts, including a negative reference to Beverly Augello as a "lying rat" cooperator. The posting included what appeared to be a nude photo of Freddy's former wife. The photo, a shot of a woman's bare back, was more artistic than pornographic, but became one of the issues in a witness-intimidation case against Kachbalian in which he eventually pled guilty.

The pretrial publicity continued into the summer of 2018, with one report in particular raising eyebrows in judicial circles. On June 22, *20/20*, ABC's prime-time newsmagazine show, devoted its entire hour-long show to the murder of April Kauffman. Carole Weintraub was at home watching with her longtime friend Jennifer Cooper, the commercial airline pilot.

On screen, Nancy Grace, a contributor on the show, made a sarcastic reference to James Kauffman, the grieving widower April left behind.

"Just fifteen months after his wife's murder, he ties the knot again," said Grace from an ABC studio.

"He remarries Carole Weintraub," Grace continued while the camera panned to a photo of the happy couple. "When did that start?" Grace snorted. "Now the version we've gotten is that they started dating after April was found murdered. Now, that's some romance."

The report went on to describe the suicide of James Kauffman: how five months earlier, just after breakfast at the Hudson County Jail, the doctor had hanged himself.

Then there was this comment from a surprising source.

"He understood that the end was near," said Atlantic County prosecutor Damon Tyner on camera. Tyner, who has declined to be interviewed for this book, apparently approved his office's participation in the *20/20* report.

The show used Tyner's comment to segue into a more startling disclosure from another ABC commentator. "Dr. Kauffman did leave something behind," a suicide note, and "this note was obtained by *20/20*."

ABC then displayed the suicide note on TV. It was addressed to Carole, but this was the first time she was seeing it. It was supposed to be under seal, a confidential piece of evidence in a murder case. But somebody had leaked it to *20/20*.

Carole recognized the handwriting; it was indeed Jimmy's. She was stunned. Television reporters and producers, she thought, had read a note that was addressed to her, a note she had yet to see.

She then watched Nancy Grace on TV ridiculing parts of the note, including quotes that her husband had written in Latin. Grace seemed to take particular glee in citing one of the Latin quotes. *"Morituri te Salutamus,"* James Kauffman had written. Literally that means, "We who are about to die salute you."

Grace claimed those were the last words of gladiators getting ready to die in ancient Rome. A more historically accurate explanation is that the statement was made to the Roman emperor Claudius by captives and criminals sentenced to die. But it was more famously used by Russell Crowe in the movie *Gladiator,* as the last words of a condemned man in the Coliseum. That was apparently where Grace got her information.

Carole Weintraub watched in shock and amazement.

There was more.

On camera, *20/20* host Deborah Roberts talked about how the April Kauffman murder had been a cold case for nearly six years until a new sheriff came to town. The TV show presented Atlantic County prosecutor Damon Tyner as a fearless crime buster who had gone after the guilty parties. If it weren't for his intervention, *20/20* was saying, people would have literally gotten away with murder. Cynical viewers had to question whether *20/20* was heaping praise on Tyner in exchange for the suicide note. The degree of cooperation between the prosecutor's office and the TV show was astounding.

ABC has never disclosed how it obtained the note. Tyner's office has denied it provided it to the network.

But on the day before the show aired, the prosecutor's office took what the *Star-Ledger* of Newark described as "the unusual step of issuing a press release about the TV exposure, noting that *20/20* host Deborah Roberts interviewed Prosecutor Damon Tyner and other members of his office."

"We are optimistic that the show will depict the hard work and effort of the women and men of ACPO [the Atlantic County Prosecutor's Office] in a favorable light," Tyner was quoted as saying in the press release, which was made public on June 21, 2018.

In addition to Tyner being interviewed on the show, Detective James Scoppa led host Deborah Roberts on a guided tour of the crime scene, throughout the Kauffman home, including the upstairs bedroom where April Kauffman was murdered.

Then a TV reporter asked Kim Pack on air why the previous Atlantic County prosecutor hadn't arrested Dr. Kauffman six years before. Pack responded that this was "the million-dollar question."

And, like the journalists at *20/20*, Pack laid a verbal bouquet at the prosecutor's feet.

"I was blessed and granted the ability to have peace in my life for the first time in six years by a man with determination . . . that believed in my story," Pack told a national TV audience. "And that was Damon Tyner. And I am forever grateful to that man."

Tyner's role in the investigation, like that of his predecessor James McClain, continues to be a subject of controversy. There are those who believe he was the driving force in solving one of the biggest murder cases in Atlantic County history. There are others who contend that he saw the investigation as a vehicle for his own personal aggrandizement and did whatever was necessary to get an indictment.

If McClain dragged his feet and overanalyzed facts and evidence, as some critics believe, then Tyner sprinted toward a preordained conclusion built around the testimony of suspect and less-than-credible witnesses.

Carole Weintraub didn't know what to believe as she watched the *20/20* report and saw a part of her life, and a man she had once loved, mocked and ridiculed.

"I absolutely broke down and cried like a baby," she said.

"Jen just put her arms around me and held me for who knows how long? I was shocked to see it on television. I thought it was a confidential document, and here it was for all the world to see.

"I felt such despair and defeat. And to hear them mocking the letter on national TV was humiliating. I am not a crier, except with hurt-animal movies, but this really just knocked the stuffing out of me. . . . I realize there is probably not a lot of sympathy for me, but I didn't and don't care. It was wrong."

Shortly after this, Judge DeLury issued a gag order barring everyone involved in the case, including the prosecutor, from commenting publicly. But Carole saw this as too little, too late. Just another example of the system failing to guarantee what she had assumed were basic rights. First, her husband had been denied bail in a case built around a weapons offense stemming from the raid on his office. Then he had been charged with murder and arbitrarily transferred to a jail hours away, and now, in death, he was being ridiculed publicly for things that he had written to her in private, things that she had not been allowed to see.

From her perspective, the *20/20* report was a hyped rush to judgment, an overblown preview of a case that would be touted as a major achievement for the Atlantic County Prosecutor's Office.

Not everyone, of course, saw it that way. There were parts of the report (especially those without the sarcastic commentary) that provided an accurate account of a successful investigation and a portrait of a troubled marriage.

And there was this from Carole's daughter, Abby, who picked up on one disturbing scene in the documentary that rang true to her. The show replayed a portion of the wedding of James and April Kauffman and captured a moment in which James Kauffman moved in to briefly pose for a perfunctory photo with April's daughter, Kim Pack. He then moved quickly away from her.

"He was always cold to me," Pack said in the *20/20* interview. "He always kept me at an arm's length."

On camera, Nancy Grace, during a slow-motion replay, pointed to James Kauffman's treatment of Kim at his wedding to April: "No hugging, no kissing, no warmth, nothing."

For Carole's daughter, Abby, that part hit very close to home. She had been there. She had felt the chill of James Kauffman.

In an interview, Abby talked about the way Kauffman treated her when her mother wasn't there. He was bossy and nasty, she said, and "would make a point of telling me he didn't want me around.

"He called me a leech. He called me a swine. He drove a wedge between me and my mom [because] he wanted her all to himself. He was a crazy psycho."

No hugging. No kissing. No warmth.

The gag order that Judge DeLury issued on July 23, 2018, applied to everyone involved in the case, including prosecutors, defense attorneys, investigators and the defendant, Freddy Augello, who had begun posting, through associates, on Facebook. Prosecutors had claimed that Augello was releasing confidential grand jury material about cooperating witnesses. Under the judge's order, the only time comments could be made would be in open court.

In addition, the judge ordered that "the parties shall take

immediate steps to remove to the greatest possible extent any materials and information that the parties have posted concerning the case that remains under their control, such as personal social media sites, and organizational or business websites within 48 hours."

That summer, as trial preparations intensified, the prosecutor's office began to line up its presentation. Glick, of course, was the key witness. He continued to be debriefed, going over the meetings he had had with Augello and listening to and explaining the taped conversations that he had made while wearing a wire for investigators.

That, of course, was behind the scenes.

Publicly, the other defendants in the case firmed up their deals, entering guilty pleas to related charges and agreeing to testify for the prosecution. Glenn "Slasher" Seeler, Cheryl Pizza, Beverly Augello, Tabitha Chapman and Joseph "Irish" Mulholland all got on board.

Mulholland, the only defendant tied directly to the murder, had quickly decided that cooperating was his only option. Like Glick, he saw no alternative. He and his attorney met with authorities after his arrest on January 9, and by March 23, he agreed to make a formal statement and enter into a cooperation agreement.

He said he had had discussions about murdering April Kauffman with both Fred Augello and James Kauffman. In fact, he said, a year before the murder the doctor offered him $100,000 to carry out the hit. This occurred, he said, when he showed up at the doctor's office for his regular pill mill visit.

Mulholland said he turned down the doctor's offer and repeatedly told both James Kauffman and Fred Augello that he wasn't interested, that he didn't want to be involved in killing a woman. "That's not my style," he would later say from the witness stand.

But he admitted that he had driven Frank Mulholland to and from the murder scene on the morning April Kauffman was shot. He claimed he did it because Fred Augello told him "if I didn't do it, I would be next."

After the murder, he said Fred would occasionally ask him, "How's the junkie doing?" and at one point discussed "taking out" Frank Mulholland. Joe Mulholland said he warned Frank to stay away from Augello, but that by that point, it was too late. Distraught over his role in the shooting of April Kauffman, Frank Mulholland "was out on a bender for a year and a half" before dying of a now-suspect drug overdose.

He also described Fred Augello's growing paranoia as the murder investigation began to close in on them. He said Augello had told him that he had people who could "take care of" James Kauffman in jail and also expressed concern about Glick, who he feared might be cooperating. He said at one point Augello pointed a gun at him, alleging that he had had something to do with the letter sent by Edwin Jacobs that identified Augello and Frank Mulholland as possible suspects in the April Kauffman murder. Joe Mulholland said Jacobs's law partner, Louis Barbone, had once represented him. Augello, in a disjointed fit of paranoia, somehow thought that tied Joe Mulholland to the accusatory letter.

The threats, fear and accusations continued even after they were arrested. When they were both in the Atlantic County Jail,

Joe Mulholland said, Fred warned him that "if you open your mouth, you're dead."

Mulholland, like all the other defendants in the case except Augello, was released on bail. His testimony at the trial in large part supported Glick's version of events and gave the prosecutor's office two witnesses who could provide detailed, firsthand accounts of a murder conspiracy.

The other defendants would be able to add bits and pieces.

In September jury selection began. It lasted a week.

On September 17, 2018, Fred Augello's trial on murder, drug-dealing and conspiracy charges opened before Judge Bernard DeLury in Atlantic County Superior Court. Augello—dressed in a suit and tie, clean-shaven, his long hair tied in a graying ponytail that stretched to the middle of his back, a small gold hoop dangling from his left earlobe—was led into courtroom five on the third floor of the criminal justice center. He was represented by two lawyers from the public defender's office, Mary Linehan and Omar Aguilar.

Augello, his glasses perched on the top of his head, nodded and smiled at several friends and family members seated in the small courtroom. It was a routine that played out almost every day for the next two weeks. Armed officers from the Atlantic County Sheriff's Office would lead him in from a side room, remove his handcuffs and the shackles around his ankles and escort him to the defense table. By the time the jury was called into the room, Augello was seated and flanked by his lawyers.

Members of the media sat on the other side of the courtroom along with some members of the prosecution support staff and, on occasion, friends of April Kauffman.

Sitting alone, often with a notepad on her lap, was Carole Weintraub. She wanted to hear for herself the evidence and testimony that painted her husband as a drug dealer and murderer.

Chief Assistant County Prosecutor Seth Levy offered the opening statement for the prosecution, laying out the theory of the case and what he told the jury the evidence and testimony would prove.

Levy said James Kauffman and Fred Augello entered into an agreement to have April Kauffman killed. Both men, Levy said, wanted to save their "empires."

Kauffman's empire, he said, was built around his thriving medical practice, his financially rewarding speaking engagements and his homes in Linwood and in Arizona.

"He was married to a beautiful, vivacious and successful wife, a woman who increased not only his practice but his fortune," Levy told the jurors. "This was Jim Kauffman's empire, and he loved it more than anything in the entire world."

But by the summer of 2011, nearly a year before the murder, "the marriage was falling apart," Levy said. There were "rumors" that April was "stepping out, having affairs." She had told friends and family members that she wanted a divorce. The prosecutor said she was embarrassed after learning that her husband had lied about being a Vietnam War hero and, he added, she had also learned about his involvement in the pill mill ring with the Pagans and threatened to expose it.

April Kauffman wanted out. And because of that she became a threat to her husband and the fortune he had amassed, Levy said. Enraged, Kauffman told her "he would kill her and her entire family before he gave her half his empire."

Murder made more financial sense than divorce.

Enter Fred Augello.

Augello's empire, the prosecutor said, was built around the pill mill operation he had going with James Kauffman and the promised cash from the murder contract. Augello was the "boss" of the drug operation, directing members of the Pagans and their associates in the scheme built around bogus prescriptions written by the doctor. Those scripts were turned into pills and cash, with Fred Augello getting the lion's share of each.

"Everyone has to pay the boss," Levy said.

Levy told the jury that it would be hard to imagine two more different people than the wealthy doctor who wanted to be part of high society and the guitar-playing, drug-dealing biker boss. But their "mutual greed" brought them together.

"They found common ground," he said. "They came together to silence April, to make sure their empires of easy money would last forever."

The prosecutor then outlined the murder plot for the jurors and provided details that he said would be presented to them as testimony from witnesses who "were not necessarily nice people."

That description, of course, could have been applied to most of the cooperators. But Levy singled out Andrew Glick in particular, telling the jury that Glick only agreed to cooperate after he was arrested on drug charges and faced a lengthy prison sentence. Levy frankly admitted that the only reason Glick was testifying was because he didn't want to go to jail. He said Glick was "a rat . . . a snitch." But, he added, "Ratting on this drug dealer, snitching on this murderer, might be the most honest, selfless thing Andrew has done his entire life."

Fred Augello's lawyers had an uphill battle going in. And their presentation, often disjointed and at times unfocused, set the tone for the two-week trial.

In her opening, Mary Linehan told the jury that the prosecution had dropped the ball in the April Kauffman investigation, that authorities had been aware of the pill mill operation and the murder plot for months before April was killed. Yet, she said, they had done nothing about it.

The case and the charges that were finally brought and that put Fred Augello at the defense table had grown out of a government effort that she likened to the bailout of American financial institutions in the wake of the great recession of 2007 to 2008.

"April Kauffman died violently . . . at the behest of her husband," she said. But the case that was going to be presented to them, and that placed Fred Augello at the heart of the conspiracy, was not built on facts and evidence. But rather, like the "too big to fail" financial bailout, it was a government effort to make up for what it had failed to do.

She said the prosecutor's office did not act for six years on the information it had received prior to April Kauffman's murder—six years, she added, while the drug ring flourished.

The national exposure—an apparent reference to the *20/20* report—had heightened the need to make the case, to present Fred Augello as James Kauffman's henchman, as the man who put the murder plot in motion. Never mind that the evidence was weak, that the witnesses were less than credible.

The defense, she told the jury, would demonstrate "what the state has done and what the state has failed to do. . . . It's time for the accounting to be done."

FIFTEEN

He didn't look like an outlaw biker when he took the stand, and that, of course, was the point. Dressed in an open-collared white shirt with sleeves that hid his tattoos, and his hair neatly trimmed, Andrew Glick was the lead witness in the murder trial of Fred Augello. And his testimony, which extended over parts of five days, established the case for the prosecution.

He was matter-of-fact about his own life of crime but highly detailed in his descriptions of his dealings with Augello. He also offered explanations about the tapes, the conversations in which the prosecution contended Augello implicated himself in the crimes for which he was being tried.

That might have been a bit of a stretch. Some of the tapes were incriminating, but they were all open to different interpretations. The jury also had to depend on Glick's account of what Augello was writing on notes while they were meeting.

"The doc was looking for someone to kill his wife," Glick said during his first day on the stand. April Kauffman wanted a divorce, and the doc "wasn't going to give her half" of his estate, said Glick. That testimony bolstered the motive for the murder presented by the prosecution. Glick said he had been told the doc was worth about five million dollars.

But he told the jury he passed on the chance to get involved in the contract killing.

"My forte is not that," he said. "It's hustling."

He was a drug dealer and an outlaw biker, he said, but not a killer.

Seth Levy then led Glick through the entire story, from his first meeting with James Kauffman, the pill mill operation, the ongoing attempts by the doc to hire a hit man, Fred Augello's role in the conspiracy and the investigation that at first appeared stalled, but that eventually led to his decision to cooperate and give it all up.

He also helped interpret the tapes that Levy introduced as evidence. He told the jury that Augello's verbal denials during several taped conversations were part of a charade that Freddy was playing. He feared listening devices and was concerned that Glick might be a cooperator.

On one tape the jury heard Augello claim that he didn't know James Kauffman. Glick said that was patently untrue and that it made no sense for Augello to say that to him because he, Augello, knew that Glick was aware of the relationship between the doc and Freddy.

"He said that for his protection," Glick said, "in case I was recording."

The notes were another way to avoid saying anything that might be used against him, Glick said, explaining that one of the first notes Augello wrote, using a black Sharpie as they sat in the front seat of his van, focused on his plan to eliminate the doc.

"Here's the deal," Augello said on the tape that rolled for the jury. "Here's what we're gonna do." Then, Glick said, Augello took his black marker and wrote, "The doc will be dead in two days." With that, Glick said, Augello folded up the note and put it in his pocket.

On cross-examination, which began on the third day of his testimony, Glick admitted he had gotten an even better deal for cooperating than he had expected. Earlier that summer all the charges pending against him had been dropped. Case dismissed. It was a sweetheart of a deal. Usually a cooperator gets credit for working with the prosecution when he appears before a judge to be sentenced. The result is usually a significant reduction in the amount of jail time warranted by the charges.

But no jail time at all? Glick hit the prosecutorial jackpot. Yet the defense did not hammer away at that point on cross-examination. Instead, he was able to continue to set the narrative, telling his story in his own words.

He readily admitted to his life as a drug trafficker, but he tap-danced around giving up the names of any of his suppliers or customers. Most bikers, he said, only knew one another by their nicknames and so he talked about "Jazz" and "Zorro" and "Jersey Jim" and "Bear" and "Shorty" and "Ace." While he might have been less than forthcoming about their real identities, he never shied away from or tried to sugarcoat his own life of crime.

He was good at what he did, and he knew how to make money. That was one of the reasons, he said, that he was able to move so quickly up the ladder and gain a leadership role in the club. But it all came apart, he admitted, on November 1, 2017, when authorities raided his home and arrested him for drug dealing.

He said he had brought his entire stash of meth and cocaine to his house on Ridge Avenue that day because he wanted to take an inventory. His plan was to put the drugs back into his stash house, "but I never had a chance . . . due to unexpected company, the police."

At the time of his arrest, he said, he had been "disillusioned and burned the hell out," so he had agreed to cooperate. Asked how often he had met with Detective Scoppa once he agreed to wear a wire, Glick replied, "More than I wanted to.

"I wasn't happy doing this," he said at another point. "I felt like a scumbag . . . [but] I had no other choice."

Glick was the linchpin in the case, and it was crucial that the jury accept his version of events. While he was on the stand, it was impossible to know what the jurors thought. But one observer who sat and listened to all his testimony came away convinced he was telling the truth.

Carole Weintraub said Glick's story, his demeanor and his frequent references to her husband as "the doc" made it clear to her that her husband had been in a "long-term situation" with Glick and the Pagans.

"It was shocking for me" to realize that, she said. "Here was this man I was living with and loved and cared for that was distributing illegal drugs."

She said after her husband's suicide, she went "on a mission" to find out if he had done the things he was accused of doing. She said she wanted—needed—answers. Glick's testimony and other evidence provided during the trial gave her some of those answers.

"What really drove it home to me in that courtroom," she said, was hearing Glick describe the drug-distribution network, how the drugs moved from person to person. His testimony, she said, was real, unvarnished and believable.

A jury would eventually agree.

Following Glick's stint on the witness stand, Levy used Joe Mulholland to provide additional details about the murder plot and what had gone down on the morning April Kauffman was shot. His testimony was later bolstered by video-surveillance footage from cameras at Mainland Regional High School about a block from the murder scene. Those video shots, authorities told the jury, showed the vehicles driven by James Kauffman and Joe Mulholland that morning and later captured the figure of a man who authorities said was Frank Mulholland walking away.

Glenn Seeler and Cheryl Pizza added details about the pill mill and talked about their troubled relationship. Seeler, who had been a member of the Pagans under both Augello and Glick, offered his take on the leadership styles of the two men.

"Andrew would take suggestions and let people have a vote," Seeler said. "Fred would just have it his way."

Beverly Augello provided more damaging testimony when

she told the jury about picking up the envelope on the morning of the murder. She also said she had purchased a burner phone for Fred Augello around the time the murder plot was being hatched.

Levy would later introduce evidence linking 276 calls between that phone and James Kauffman's office. There were 103 calls from Kauffman's office to the burner phone and 173 calls from the burner phone to the office. There were no other numbers ever called by the burner phone, investigators said. The last call was the day before April Kauffman was killed. From that point on, there was no further communication between the two phones.

April Kauffman's handyman, Billy Gonzalez, described finding "Miss April" sprawled on the floor that morning and told of the frantic phone call he had received from James Kauffman.

And several of April's friends testified about her rocky marriage and described the controlling nature of the doctor.

One witness said several of April's girlfriends referred to James Kauffman as "Perimeter Pete" because he was "obsessive about security," always making sure the doors were locked. This was clearly at odds with the door being left unlocked on the morning of the murder. She also recalled seeing large sums of cash, usually wads of twenty-dollar bills, around the house.

Another said James Kauffman could be "sweet and endearing" but then turn "vicious and nasty" and said April had told her that he had said "he would kill her before he would give her half his empire."

One of the final witnesses called by Levy was Kim Pack,

who offered an inside look at the troubled marriage that was at the heart of the case.

Pack, repeating many of the things she had said in her sworn but not publicly disclosed deposition testimony in the civil case, said that her mother "was done with him and wanted a divorce" but that James Kauffman refused.

Instead, she believed, he had found another way to end their marriage.

Closing arguments were heard on October 2, 2018, setting the stage for what some observers felt would be lengthy jury deliberations.

In his summation, Levy painted Augello as the mastermind of the pill mill and the expediter of the murder.

"When you move the pawns out of the way, all you have staring back at you is 'Freddy Crime World,' 'Miserable,' Ferdinand Augello," Levy said. "The leader of a racketeering organization, hands dripping red with the blood of April Kauffman."

Mary Linehan, during her final statements to the jury, argued that the prosecution had failed to prove its case and that while her client might have "talked big," he lacked the money, means and opportunity to get anything done. She told the jury that the case was built on the unreliable testimony of witnesses who were trying to get out from under their own criminal problems, witnesses who had cut deals with the government and were willing to say whatever the prosecution wanted.

She called the case "prosecution by multiple choice."

The jury wasn't buying it.

It took the seven women and five men who were sitting in

judgment of Fred Augello a little more than two hours to reach a verdict. Augello was found guilty of every charge.

He sat stoically as the jury verdicts were announced, his somber attitude in contrast to the optimistic thumbs-up he had given to supporters after Linehan had finished her summation a few hours earlier.

Kim Pack sobbed in the first row of the courtroom as the verdicts were announced. It was, she would later say, the culmination of a nearly six-year battle to find justice.

Damon Tyner told reporters that while justice might not have been swift, "it was fair." And he said it was his hope "that April's family will now be able to find some measure of peace, knowing that those responsible for their loved one's death have all been punished in one form or another."

He said James Kauffman had been tried "by a higher jury."

"It cost him his life. He couldn't live with the weight of the evidence that would have been presented against him on this date. . . . I think of his role in flooding the market with oxycodone. His legacy is all of the tragedy he left behind, the lives that were lost, and the people who were affected by his mispractice of medicine."

Several months later James Kauffman's lawyer, Edwin Jacobs, had a different take on the way the case played out. In most legal circles, the consensus is that had Kauffman been alive and had he gone to trial with Jacobs as his attorney, the case would have taken on a decidedly different look.

If nothing else, Jacobs would have aggressively challenged the testimony of cooperating witnesses like Andrew Glick and

Joe Mulholland, a technique he had mastered and used successfully in several high-profile organized-crime cases. Mob boss
Joseph "Skinny Joey" Merlino was found not guilty of murder
in a federal case in Philadelphia and in another in Newark with
Jacobs as his lawyer.

Jacobs said he was amazed that all the charges against Glick
were dropped, that he faced no jail time despite his arrest on
drug-dealing and weapons offenses, charges that Glick himself
had said could have sent him to prison for forty years.

"All the charges against Glick just disappeared," Jacobs said.
"It's a good deal [for him]."

But was it a good deal for the public?

"I have said for decades from my perspective as a criminal
attorney, it is wrong for prosecutors to give cooperating witnesses a free pass," Jacobs said. "I think it's overused and
abused. . . . I always thought it was wrong to let people off. . . .
I think it's wrong for prosecutors to be able to absolve people
facing serious charges. . . . Generally, I think it's not in the public interest to let people off scot-free."

The obvious risk, Jacobs said, is that the "guy telling the
story might be making it up" in order to "benefit" himself.

Jacobs also said that he would have liked the chance to defend James Kauffman in open court and that had he gone to
trial, he would have put Kauffman on the stand. The stolen-
valor issue might have presented some problems, he said, but
that was a chance he was willing to take.

"I feel bad that we didn't get a chance. We had no platform
to show a jury that we were innocent," Jacobs said, "and dem-

onstrate to a jury that the claims being made against him by motivated plea-bargained witnesses and the charges that were being leveled by prosecutors weren't correct."

Kauffman and Augello at the same defense table, of course, would have created a different set of problems. Each might have accused the other of the murder, making a joint defense nearly impossible. A more probable scenario would have been separate trials. All of that became moot, however, when James Kauffman was found dead in his Hudson County Jail cell.

While he had opted not to testify in his own defense, Fred Augello did have some parting words as he was led out of the courtroom on the afternoon the jury found him guilty.

"This is for the media: I did not kill Mrs. Kauffman, nor did I pay anyone to kill Mrs. Kauffman," he said. It was a stance that Augello had taken throughout the trial, and one that continues today as his appeal process winds its way through the court system.

SIXTEEN

On December 5, 2018, Ferdinand Augello was sentenced to life plus thirty years. That sentence, absent a successful appeal, means the biker, who was sixty-two at the time, will die in prison.

At his sentencing hearing, Augello took the opportunity to lay out his version of events, insisting that he had had nothing to do with the murder or the pill mill ring. Dressed in an orange prison jumpsuit, his glasses again perched on the top of his head, Augello asked that his handcuffs be removed before he addressed the court. His request was granted.

What followed was a rambling thirty-minute soliloquy.

He called the case "a farce." He told the judge, "I'm not John Gotti." There had been no drug ring, he said, but rather "a drug-addict ring," a group of drug addicts who "ate" the pills that Jim Kauffman prescribed. He said the drug operation had been controlled by Andrew Glick, one of the chief witnesses against him, and the murder had been set in motion by Joseph Mulholland, his other chief accuser.

Both men, he said, had had reasons to lie and to implicate him in order to avoid their own prosecutions. He offered to take a lie-detector test. He said the case "has nothing to do with the Pagan's Motorcycle Club" and insisted that he had not known Frank Mulholland. He said he "never gave anyone any money to kill anybody."

He said he felt "horrible" for what happened to April Kauffman and sorry for Kim Pack, who had made an emotional statement about the death of her mother and the impact it had had on her and her children before Augello rose to speak.

"But I'm not the guy," Augello said, again claiming that Joseph Mulholland was responsible for the murder and also for the overdose death of Frank Mulholland.

"Him and his creepy cousin killed April Kauffman," Augello said, sticking to the false assumption that the Mulhollands were related. "And then he killed his creepy cousin.

"I'm the fall guy," he said. "I'm amazed it got this far. . . . I didn't murder Mrs. Kauffman. I didn't send anybody to kill Mrs. Kauffman. It's just a bunch of nonsense. . . . The real murderer is dead, and the other guy is sitting home, watching TV."

And Andrew Glick, he added, is "buying hookers" and selling dope.

"Everything I've said is the damn truth," he said. "I'm not an angel, but . . . I did not murder April Kauffman. And I'm going to prison for the rest of my life. It's just unbelievable."

While the verdict and sentencing offered Damon Tyner a

chance to take a victory lap, his achievement in the April Kauffman murder investigation was already under a cloud by the time Augello stood up in court that day.

On November 5, 2018, Carole Weintraub filed a grievance against him with the Office of Attorney Ethics, a division of the New Jersey Supreme Court set up to investigate complaints about the conduct of lawyers practicing in the Garden State.

In the complaint, she wrote, "Damon Tyner violated my civil rights by disclosing [the suicide note] addressed to my lawyer and myself only to the national ABC program on *20/20*. The letter was displayed and contents discussed before a national audience not once but twice because the program was played a second time."

Carole said she had been trying from January 2018 to obtain the letter but had been rebuffed by the court because of the pending murder trial. To display the note on national television, she said, was "totally out of bounds ethically." She accused Tyner of releasing her "private property for public consumption and self-aggrandizement."

At this writing, her complaint is still being investigated. She has been told the process could take a year or more.

Meanwhile, ABC did some editing, perhaps to cover its tracks. On its website, as well as on *20/20* videos posted on YouTube, the show's praise of Tyner, as well as most of his on-camera interview, has been edited out.

A month after the Augello sentencing, the prosecutor came under fire again. This time in a whistle-blower lawsuit filed on January 10, 2019, in Atlantic County Superior Court, by three women who were formerly high-ranking employees in the prosecutor's office.

The plaintiffs, former First Assistant Prosecutor Diane Ruberton, former Chief Assistant Prosecutor Donna Fetzer, and Heather McManus, a former lieutenant of county investigators, sued Tyner, his first assistant, the prosecutor's office and the county, charging Tyner with gender discrimination, mortgage fraud, official misconduct, unlawful retaliation, and violations of their civil rights.

The suit alleged that Tyner had created a "toxic culture" that included turning "a blind eye to instances and reports of sexual harassment and gender discrimination, and permitted retaliation against anyone who dared question this culture and/or the perceived unlawful activities of Defendant Tyner."

In response, Tyner denied the allegations. His lawyers filed a motion to dismiss the entire complaint, saying it was "immaterial, redundant, scandalous and/or impertinent," but the judge in the case twice denied that motion.

Carole Weintraub found the lawsuit fascinating because it charged Tyner with unethical dealings with the media during the April Kauffman murder case.

It alleged that the prosecutor "seized an opportunity afforded by this high-profile murder case to aggrandize himself before the media, including an interview with ABC's *20/20* TV show," adding that his "publicity tour earned him an admonishment from a state Superior Court judge because Defendant Tyner's tour occurred while charges against defendants in the Kauffman case were pending."

The lawsuit also alleged that during the Kauffman murder investigation Tyner's office learned that a local police officer might have leaked information indicating Andrew Glick was cooperating, but that despite office guidelines that required an internal investigation, "Tyner took no action."

The most damaging charges in the lawsuit involved an alleged "phantom sale" by Tyner that the suit contended amounted to bank fraud. According to the lawsuit, Tyner and his wife bought a home in Egg Harbor Township in 2003 for $275,819, and then, three years later, sold it to Tyner's father-in-law for $425,000. But Tyner and his family maintained the house as their primary residence. Six months after the sale, Tyner's father-in-law sold the house back to Tyner for one dollar. Tyner then remortgaged the home, borrowing $417,000 on a house valued at $270,000, before defaulting.

Finally, the suit charged that Tyner threatened to fire McManus and Fetzer because they raised issues consistent with "the public policy of New Jersey to close the gender wage gap" and fired Ruberton after demoting her and cutting her pay by $20,000.

Ruberton, of course, was the acting prosecutor after Jim McClain was appointed a judge by Governor Chris Christie. By most accounts, she had been expected to succeed McClain. However, Christie, a Republican, opted to appoint Tyner, a Democrat. Politics clearly played a role in that appointment, and those who support Tyner claim the whistle-blower lawsuit was merely political sour grapes.

Any changes Tyner made in the office after he took over, those supporters say, were motivated by standard political considerations—Democrats promote Democrats just as Republicans promote Republicans—and had nothing to do with gender issues.

An equally important question as the suit moves through the court system is what, if any, impact it might have on Augello's case. Some of the issues raised in the civil litigation relate to the investigation and prosecution. It will be up to Augello's lawyers to demonstrate whether those alleged improprieties tainted the conviction.

For Augello's codefendants, on the other hand, there was no turning back.

Joseph "Irish" Mulholland got hit the hardest at sentencing. Despite mini-testimonials from nearly a dozen people who showed up to speak on his behalf, he was sentenced to four years in state prison by Judge DeLury.

Mulholland, who drove the hit man to and from the murder scene and who admitted pocketing a thousand dollars for his trouble, told DeLury, "I'm sorry I got involved with what I got involved with."

A recovering drug addict, Mulholland had cleaned up his act, was in a rehabilitation program for drug abusers and was hoping for less jail time, perhaps a suspended sentence. He was described by one supporter as "a shining example of how it works in the program."

But he was also an example of how the judicial system usually works. Andrew Glick got an extraordinarily exceptional deal. Mulholland's was more in line with how the process typically works. He had pleaded guilty to a racketeering charge that could have carried a ten-year sentence, perhaps even more. Four years was a break, a decent deal and, in most law enforcement circles, the sentence was considered adequate recognition for his cooperation.

Glenn Seeler was the only other cooperator to get jail time. He was sentenced to three years in state prison after pleading guilty, like Mulholland, to a second-degree racketeering charge.

"I've changed," he told the judge, according to a news account of his sentencing that appeared in the *Press of Atlantic City*. "I'm sorry about the past, I really am. There's nothing more I can say or do. I've done everything in my power to make amends." His estranged wife, Cheryl Pizza, got a three-year suspended sentence. Beverly Augello, whose limited but pointed testimony helped make the case, got a five-year suspended sentence.

And Tabitha Chapman was admitted into a pretrial intervention program that would allow her record to be cleared if she avoided any brushes with the law for a year. At her sentencing her lawyer said she had been "victimized" by Fred Augello.

Paul Pagano, the only Augello codefendant who opted not to cooperate, eventually pleaded guilty to a disorderly conduct charge and got no jail time. Glick said he had told authorities all along that Pagano was not part of a pill mill operation. Any drugs he received were for personal use.

"He ate all the pills the doc prescribed for him," Glick said, "including some pills he bought from me."

In May 2019 John "the Egyptian" Kachbalian appeared before DeLury after pleading guilty to attempted witness tampering. The ex-Pagan got no jail time. Instead, he was given a suspended 364-day sentence and four years' probation.

The sentences capped the Atlantic County pill mill investigation, a probe that offered a brief look into the opioid crisis that continues to rip America apart. In the greater scheme of things, the Kauffman-Augello operation was decidedly minor league.

In April 2019, US Justice Department officials announced the arrests of sixty doctors and pharmacists charged in a massive illegal opioid operation.

"Some of the doctors are accused of trading drugs for sex, giving prescriptions to Facebook friends without proper medical exams and unnecessarily pulling teeth to justify writing pain pill prescriptions," according to a report in the *Cincinnati Enquirer.*

The case involved twenty-eight thousand patients and three hundred fifty thousand improper prescriptions filled in Ohio, Kentucky, Tennessee, West Virginia and Alabama, according to charges stemming from a Justice Department strike force investigation started in 2018 and aimed at the opioid epidemic.

Many of the doctors "are simply white-coated drug dealers," said J. Douglas Overbey, US Attorney in the Eastern District of Tennessee, in announcing the arrests.

According to the *Enquirer* report, more than two hundred thousand people died from overdoses related to prescription opioids from 1999 to 2017 in the United States.

April Kauffman's death would not be included in that number. But her murder was nonetheless tied to the epidemic and the greed and wanton disregard for human life that are a part of the massive American pill mill crisis.

SEVENTEEN

On December 20, 2018, fifteen days after Augello was sentenced, Carole Weintraub received the autopsy results from the New Jersey Department of Health on the death of her husband.

It was the first official document she received, and it came nearly a year after he died. The report stated that on March 10, 2018, Junaid R. Shaikh, a forensic pathologist, had determined that the cause of death was hanging and that the death was a suicide. The body was determined to be James Kauffman's by comparing the remains to his New Jersey driver's license photo.

The report said that the deceased weighed 177 pounds and was five feet five inches in height and that his remains were consistent with a man sixty-eight years old. He wore green prison pants and white boxer shorts. His hair was gray, and he had a mustache and beard at the time of his death.

The pathologist found binding marks around the doctor's throat from the hanging, and hemorrhages of the face, eyes and mouth, but "no evidence of trauma to the head, torso and extremities."

About a month later, Judge DeLury finally decided to lift the protective order on the suicide note and release it to Carole and her lawyers. It took a while for the note to be delivered to the office of Jacobs & Barbone in Atlantic City. The lawyers then forwarded it to Carole.

"It only took thirteen months to get what belonged to me," she said with a trace of bitterness.

She received it on February 14, 2019, Valentine's Day.

The note, written on yellow legal pad paper, had been found on James Kauffman's prison cell bed on the day he died. On the cover page, in handwriting Carole quickly recognized, was the notation:

> *These 6 yellow pages are for my attorney and my wife. Thank you in advance for your help.*
>
> *Sincerely,*
> *JMK MD*

James Kauffman's final words followed. And like so much else about the case, his farewell raised more questions than it answered. For cynics, and Carole was hard-pressed not to include herself among them, this was his last attempt to spin the story, to manipulate the situation, to dictate terms. Even from the grave, he was a control freak.

The signature would puzzle Carole and Jim Kauffman's doctor friends, because Kauffman was a DO, a doctor of osteopathy, and not an MD, a doctor of medicine, and he would never have made that mistake.

Conspiracy theorists—and there remain many around this case—saw it as a cryptic last message from the doc. Was he trying to indicate that he was forced to write the note under duress? Or was it just one last inside joke?

The letter opened this way:

> As G-D is my witness and will be I cannot live
> like this. I, no matter what anybody says, I did not
> do anything to my wife and I am not, was not in the
> "rackets." I am almost 69 years old + I have tried to
> live a moral, ethical + professional life. I have
> helped a lot of people and I feel good about that.
>
> Thank you for your kindness in my hopefully
> short stay.
>
> I love my wife Carole so much it truly hurts to do
> this.

Then came three quotes in Latin, a language he had studied since high school and was quite proficient in.

There was, of course, *"Morituri te Salutamus,"* the quote that Nancy Grace on *20/20* jumped on. The second Latin quote, *"ORA Pro Nobis,"* was one that any former Catholic altar boy can tell you means "Pray for us." The final Latin quote was the most chilling: *"De mortuis Nil Nisi bonum"*—"Of the dead nothing but good is to be said." The note was signed "J M Kauffman."

Replete with shorthand abbreviations, the rest of the note read this way:

> *If you read the following pages it will become self-evident. I am not blaming April. We were both stupid + naïve. What I did I was forced to do for my family so help me G-D.*
>
> *April + I decided together not to go to the police as she really felt that they no matter what they say could not have protected our family!*
>
> *I do not have audio or video to record my deathbed statement. It is the truth, the whole truth, and nothing but the truth.*
>
> *Sometime in 2011 April came to me + said would I like to go to a motorcycle rally at Smithville to meet some of her friends. When we got there they were sitting on an outside patio next to the bar. I was slightly shocked to say the least that they had the colors of Pagans! I was very nervous.*
>
> *One of the leaders said for me to see his motorcycle. When we got there he said April said I would help them out. I didn't understand + he said April would explain. We left about 1 hour later + when we got home she said that they needed a doctor who was not judgmental and they had no insurance. I said if they were her friends I would see a couple for medical problems.*
>
> *The first patients came in gradually and without colors and were very nice. They had diseases such as*

diabetes mellitus which I deal with. I did not charge them and gave them free samples for their diseases. Slowly but surely several more came. I talked to April and she said not to worry that she was getting compensated. I thought that meant they were frequenting her restaurant to give her business a boost. I found out later that money had changed hands. April told me about this later.

Shortly thereafter after hours they came in and said they wanted more narcotic scripts. I said I could not do this + a gun was shoved in my face + said April and I would be killed if I didn't. They said they were stopping the payments to April. After having diarrhea and vomiting I went home + April was crying. She said they told her the same things they told me. They also said if we went to the police or anybody else they would kill her daughter Kim + then us. It wouldn't matter who found out they would kill us. Both of us decided to keep it to ourselves.

I started to receive lots of phone calls from some phone numbers but never usually the same person. They were cajoling, threatening, demanding, etc. . . . I was and still am extremely frightened about what they can do.

I continued until about April when I said I didn't want to lose my medical license. They said I had to or face the consequences. I heard nothing but threats up until May 9th. On May 10th, after I left the

*hospital, WaWa + my office they cold-bloodedly
murdered her. April always told me to leave the door
open with the 'come in' sign on the door so if she was
in the shower she would tell them to come in + wait.
I should never have listened to that. After her death I
could not believe (naïve me) that people would think
that I did it.*

*I could not sleep or eat + keep looking over my
shoulder. I saw people staring at me + not
sitting next to me. It was awful. After work I could
not get home fast enough. I took as many out of
town speaking trips as I could so as not to be
around.*

*Six to eight weeks after the death a person named
Carole Weintraub called + left a message. She was
my high school/college girlfriend and I had not seen
or heard from her in 40+ years. We started to go out.
Because I felt comfortable with her. Professional
friends (Drs = lawyers) told me go out + be happy.
Since I wasn't twenty anymore, we did and about
one and ½ years later we got married. It was like
restarting where we left off. It was very comfortable
with her and I was and am happy to have her. She is
absolutely wonderful.*

*The bastards somehow found about it + told me
they would kill her + her daughter. They have
better sources than the authorities. I continued
to my dismay with the prescriptions. Surprisingly*

*over half were 100% legitimate if you look at the
charts.*

*I continued this pattern but did not get any call
after the death (murder). Instead, they came in
person at the visits to my office. I was told I was
being watched. "So don't try to get away with
something." I know what that meant. I am sure April
isn't the first person they had killed.*

*Approximately three years go by and they show up
after office hours while I am doing paperwork. They
took me essentially forcefully in a car to a bar
somewhere in the "sticks." It was totally filled with
Pagans. I thought this was it. They were tired of me
and I was going to be killed. I didn't drink. But they
did + some guy named 'Freddie?' came up to
me + said he wanted to be a patient + that if I didn't
he would do to me what he + some person named
Mulholland and a certain driver did to April. He also
said not to worry as Mulholland was dead + a gun was
in 3 pieces in 3 states. He said he had an affair with
April + when she broke it off the murder occurred.*

*I was beyond scared + said if he wanted to be a
patient I needed a driver's license. He did + said he
would collect it at the visit which had to be after
hours + no chart.*

James Kauffman then returned to the threats mentioned in
his earlier letter to Carole.

I kept this to myself until last year. (Mr. E. Jacobs has date) When I was getting in my car in the closed garage + was assaulted by two men who threw me face down on the concrete + put a gun to the back of my head + cocked the hammer. I am embarrassed to say I urinated in my pants as I thought I was dead. They left, I got changed + went to work and emailed my lawyer's office. We decided not to open a can of worms so the police were not called. (Mr. Jacobs was not privy to the present information about being forced to do an illegal act.)

Several weeks (maybe a month) went by + I got nervous that they would kill me on the road. I then got a small pistol when I went from the house to the office + back and dutifully removed it at one of the 2 premises except for June 13!!!! Dumb me . . .

Some time later I went to see Mr. Jacobs + gave him the 2 names I had collected. After some period of time, we decided to give it to the prosecutor's office for him to follow that lead and arrest the real killers. I couldn't understand why nothing was done . . . I was doubly stunned on Tuesday with the new charges + that I had to move to a distant jail.

This left me with no choice but to do what I am going to do now. I see those dirt bags ganged up to save their butts while frying mine. To those who think that is a fabrication or prevarication, I put my money where my mouth is.

I'm Dead!

*And as another person said: Forgive them father
(the doubters) know not what they do!*

*I want to apologize to any person I have hurt,
insulted or was rude to in my 68 plus years.
Especially to my wife Carole + her daughter Abb.
I made peace with God and said the Schima.
I'm ready to go. Goodbye.*

*P.S. Sorry about my handwriting and thanks to my
friends who stood by me. They knew I didn't kill
April.*

For Carole, the suicide note was wrenching and left her wondering what to believe.

"He ended the letter with a very holy and important prayer
in Hebrew," she said. "He was all right with his God and said
he loved me and that was the end of the letter.

"I'd like to believe that he loved me, but I can't come to terms
with what happened because I don't know what's true and I
don't know what's untrue," she said.

She said a friend has told her that she had to "put the anger
away," but she admitted she couldn't. The ambiguity, the ab-
sence of truth, constantly gnaws at her.

And so does a feeling of guilt by association.

"My general feeling is I can't get the stink off of me," she
said. "I mean it just that way. It follows me all the time. Even in
the most mundane ways it follows me."

If she could talk to her husband, she said she would say,
"Tell me the truth, Jimmy. Please, just tell me the unvarnished,

ugly truth. I need to know. I want to know. I don't need any embellishments. I just want to know what happened."

Instead, she's left with the suicide note, a rambling account of events often at odds with the testimony and evidence presented at the murder trial and, according to Andrew Glick at least, a total fabrication.

Carole has tried to analyze her husband's final words and believes the note began on a false premise, that he and April were young and naïve.

"Jimmy was many things, but he was not naïve," she said. "He was the kind of guy who didn't trust anybody." He was a guy who always "suspected ulterior motives in people."

She also says she does not buy his account of being threatened. Instead, she believes his involvement with the Pagans was a part of a mutually beneficial relationship. And while Glick would argue that the doc seduced Freddy Augello with the promise of drugs and cash, Carole thinks it was her husband who was seduced by the Pagans.

"I think it was gradual, a seduction, very well thought out," she said, adding that for the Pagans, "It wasn't their first rodeo."

She said when she first asked her husband about the outlaw motorcycle gang and his ties to it, he jumped at the chance to tell her.

"It was almost like he was bragging about it," she said. As if "I'm in league with these bikers and I'm helping them, and I'm the cool guy."

"And then it escalated," she said. "That's when I think the threats came. But I think it started innocent enough."

All of that has led her reluctantly to the conclusion that James

Kauffman, the man she married, the man who was her first love, had his wife April murdered.

"I think he was involved," she said.

And then the lying began, both to avoid arrest and to create a new world and a new life with her.

"In one sense he was protecting me by telling me he was not involved," she said. But she is also reminded of what her therapist said about Jimmy, which she characterized the following way:

"He was a straight-up sociopath who played fast and loose with the truth and was mentally ill. He made life conform to his idea of the facts . . . no conscience. He bent the truth to benefit himself."

Her daughter, Abby, was quick to agree and pulled no punches in her own analysis of the last words and actions of James Kauffman.

"Committing suicide was his way of saying 'fuck you' to everybody," said Abby, who has no doubts about Kauffman's involvement in the murder of April.

That belief, Abby said, sparked an intense exchange with her own mother.

"Mom," Abby said she told Carole, "you realize this could have been you? I could have had to bury you? Do you realize the danger you put both of us in?"

"I'm sorry. I'm sorry," Carole said as she broke into tears.

"She was crying like a baby," Abby remembered. "I do thank the Lord that I didn't lose my mother. I want her to forgive herself because she's just as innocent as April was and Kim was. As I am.

"I do think she's going to be okay," Abby said. "But he

[Kauffman] knocked her down to nothing, and she's gonna have to build herself up again."

Carole has already begun the process.

She has shut down her business and gone to work for local charities. She volunteers to do things such as cooking for shut-ins.

"I have to push myself out the door," she said. "I have to make myself do things. I think it would be pretty easy for me if I just curled up and read books and watched TV for the rest of my life."

And when she does get out, she stays away from her hometown.

"I don't even come to Atlantic City," she said. "I hate it. I hate what they did to it. . . . It was a dirty little town, and it's still a dirty little town."

Carole said she doesn't think she'll ever get married again and worries about what she might become.

"I don't want to lose my sense of humor," she said, adding that she fears that what she has experienced could turn her into a "a cynical, untrusting, uncaring, not compassionate person."

Besides the urn she still keeps in the guest room of her condo, she has one last tie left to Jimmy.

His mother, now ninety-five, lives in a rest home.

Every few months, Carole visits Ruth Kauffman to check up on her physical and financial well-being. Ruth is in the final stages of dementia. She's spoken only once about her son, whom she called Jimmy, and talked about as if he were still alive.

Carole didn't say anything to change her mind.

Carole is Ruth's legal guardian. She has power of attorney. And she has no plans to change that.

Most times when she visits, Ruth doesn't know who she is.

That's the way Carole feels when she thinks about her late husband.

She has been scarred by what happened. And every day she wrestles with the fundamental questions that linger. She wonders if she ever really knew who Jimmy Kauffman was. And she's haunted by the fact that she will never know why he did what he did.

EPILOGUE

Andrew Glick was facing a different type of identity crisis. He knew who he was. But he wasn't sure whom he was about to become.

By the spring of 2019, he was still living in the Atlantic County area but had plans to leave. He had sold his house on Ridge Avenue, had banked the cash he made from the sale and was waiting on New Jersey authorities to arrange a new identity. Once he had that in place, he intended to leave the area, head either south or west. Wherever he ended up, he hoped to find a job as a cook and start a new life.

He said he will continue riding his motorcycle, but wherever he settles, he knows he will have to steer clear of biker bars and outlaw motorcycle groups. It's a close-knit world, and it would be virtually impossible for him to reestablish himself in that environment.

Regretfully, he says, his days as a Pagan are over.

With that in mind, he traveled to New York City one day in May to meet with members of a documentary company that hoped to put together a series on the pill mill murder. With the cameras rolling, Glick visited a tattoo parlor where he had his Pagans tattoo "adjusted." His right arm, from shoulder to elbow, is no longer a billboard for the club and his affiliation with it.

Instead, he now sports a massive conflagration of colors and swirls.

"It's like my life as a Pagan," he said. "Up in flames."

INDEX

George Anastasia was the mob writer at the *Philadelphia Inquirer* for years and is the author of six books on true crime. He is the recipient of numerous journalism awards and has worked on and been featured in a number of television documentaries, the most recent being a four-part series for the History Channel titled *Kingpin* that profiled the lives of John Gotti, James "Whitey" Bulger, Pablo Escobar, and Joaquín "El Chapo" Guzmán.

Ralph Cipriano is an award-winning veteran muckraking reporter who has exposed corruption in city and county governments, the Philadelphia DA's office, local police departments, Ivy League football programs, and the Catholic Church. He's the author of three books: *Courtroom Cowboy*, *The Hit Man*, and *Target: The Senator*. His book on former mob hit man–turned–government witness John Veasey was the basis for a *60 Minutes* profile of Veasey in 2013.

Ready to find
your next great read?

Let us help.

Visit prh.com/nextread

Penguin
Random
House